MACMILLAN MASTER GUIDES

GENERAL EDITOR: JAMES GIBSON

Published

JANE AUSTEN	*Emma*
	Sense
	Pride
	Mans
SAMUEL BECKETT	*Waitin*
WILLIAM BLAKE	*Songs of Innocence* and *Songs of Experience* Alan Tomlinson
ROBERT BOLT	*A Man for all Seasons* Leonard Smith
EMILY BRONTË	*Wuthering Heights* Hilda D. Spear
GEOFFREY CHAUCER	*The Miller's Tale* Michael Alexander
	The Pardoner's Tale Geoffrey Lester
	The Prologue to the Canterbury Tales Nigel Thomas and Richard Swan
CHARLES DICKENS	*Bleak House* Dennis Butts
	Great Expectations Dennis Butts
	Hard Times Norman Page
GEORGE ELIOT	*Middlemarch* Graham Handley
	Silas Marner Graham Handley
	The Mill on the Floss Helen Wheeler
HENRY FIELDING	*Joseph Andrews* Trevor Johnson
E. M. FORSTER	*Howards End* Ian Milligan
	A Passage to India Hilda D. Spear
WILLIAM GOLDING	*The Spire* Rosemary Sumner
	Lord of the Flies Raymond Wilson
OLIVER GOLDSMITH	*She Stoops to Conquer* Paul Ranger
THOMAS HARDY	*The Mayor of Casterbridge* Ray Evans
	Tess of the D'Urbervilles James Gibson
	Far from the Madding Crowd Colin Temblett-Wood
JOHN KEATS	*Selected Poems* John Garrett
PHILIP LARKIN	*The Whitsun Weddings* and *The Less Deceived* Andrew Swarbrick
D. H. LAWRENCE	*Sons and Lovers* R. P. Draper
HARPER LEE	*To Kill a Mockingbird* Jean Armstrong
CHRISTOPHER MARLOWE	*Doctor Faustus* David A. Male
THE METAPHYSICAL POETS	Joan van Emden

MACMILLAN MASTER GUIDES

THOMAS MIDDLETON and WILLIAM ROWLEY	*The Changeling* Tony Bromham
ARTHUR MILLER	*The Crucible* Leonard Smith
GEORGE ORWELL	*Animal Farm* Jean Armstrong
WILLIAM SHAKESPEARE	*Richard II* Charles Barber
	Hamlet Jean Brooks
	King Lear Francis Casey
	Henry V Peter Davison
	The Winter's Tale Diana Devlin
	Julius Caesar David Elloway
	Macbeth David Elloway
	Measure for Measure Mark Lilly
	Henry IV Part I Helen Morris
	Romeo and Juliet Helen Morris
	The Tempest Kenneth Pickering
	A Midsummer Night's Dream Kenneth Pickering
GEORGE BERNARD SHAW	*St Joan* Leonée Ormond
RICHARD SHERIDAN	*The School for Scandal* Paul Ranger
	The Rivals Jeremy Rowe
ALFRED TENNYSON	*In Memoriam* Richard Gill
JOHN WEBSTER	*The White Devil* and *The Duchess of Malfi* David A. Male

Forthcoming

CHARLOTTE BRONTË	*Jane Eyre* Robert Miles
JOHN BUNYAN	*The Pilgrim's Progress* Beatrice Batson
JOSEPH CONRAD	*The Secret Agent* Andrew Mayne
T. S. ELIOT	*Murder in the Cathedral* Paul Lapworth
	Selected Poems Andrew Swarbrick
GERARD MANLEY HOPKINS	*Selected Poems* R. Watt
BEN JONSON	*Volpone* Michael Stout
RUDYARD KIPLING	*Kim* Leonée Ormond
ARTHUR MILLER	*Death of a Salesman* Peter Spalding
JOHN MILTON	*Comus* Tom Healy
WILLIAM SHAKESPEARE	*Othello* Tony Bromham
	As You Like It Kiernan Ryan
	Coriolanus Gordon Williams
	Antony and Cleopatra Martin Wine
ANTHONY TROLLOPE	*Barchester Towers* Ken Newton
VIRGINIA WOOLF	*To the Lighthouse* John Mepham
	Mrs Dalloway Julian Pattison
W. B. YEATS	*Selected Poems* Stan Smith

MACMILLAN MASTER GUIDES
RICHARD II
BY WILLIAM SHAKESPEARE

CHARLES BARBER

with an Introduction by
HAROLD BROOKS

MACMILLAN
EDUCATION

First edition 1987

Published by
MACMILLAN EDUCATION LTD
Houndmills, Basingstoke, Hampshire RG21 2XS
and London
Companies and representatives
throughout the world

Typeset in Great Britain by
TEC SET, Wallington, Surrcy

Printed in Hong Kong

Barber, Charles
Richard II by William Shakespeare. —
(Macmillan master guides)
1. Shakespeare, William. Richard II
I. Title   II. Shakespeare, William.
Richard II
822.3'3   PR2820
ISBN 0–333–41669–4 Pbk
ISBN 0–333–41670–8 Pbk export

CONTENTS

ACKNOWLEDGEMENTS

Cover illustration: a detail from *The Wilton Diptych*. Reproduced by courtesy of the Trustees of The National Gallery, London. The drawing of the Globe Theatre is by courtesy of Alec Pearson

GENERAL EDITOR'S PREFACE

The aim of the Macmillan Master Guides is to help you to appreciate the book you are studying by providing information about it and by suggesting ways of reading and thinking about it which will lead to a fuller understanding. The section on the writer's life and background has been designed to illustrate those aspects of the writer's life which have influenced the work, and to place it in its personal and literary context. The summaries and critical commentary are of special importance in that each brief summary of the action is followed by an examination of the significant critical points. The space which might have been given to repetitive explanatory notes has been devoted to a detailed analysis of the kind of passage which might confront you in an examination. Literary criticism is concerned with both the broader aspects of the work being studied and with its detail. The ideas which meet us in reading a great work of literature, and their relevance to us today, are an essential part of our study, and our Guides look at the thought of their subject in some detail. But just as essential is the craft with which the writer has constructed his work of art, and this may be considered under several technical headings — characterisation, language, style and stagecraft, for example.

The authors of these Guides are all teachers and writers of wide experience, and they have chosen to write about books they admire and know well in the belief that they can communicate their admiration to you. But you yourself must read and know intimately the book you are studying. No one can do that for you. You should see this book as a lamp-post. Use it to shed light, not to lean against. If you know your text and know what it is saying about life, and how it says it, then you will enjoy it, and there is no better way of passing an examination in literature.

JAMES GIBSON

AN INTRODUCTION TO THE STUDY OF SHAKESPEARE'S PLAYS

A play as a work of art exists to the full only when performed. It must hold the audience's attention throughout the performance, and, unlike a novel, it can't be put down and taken up again. It is important to experience the play as if you are seeing it on the stage for the first time, and you should begin by reading it straight through. Shakespeare builds a play in dramatic units which may be divided into smaller subdivisions, or episodes, marked off by exits and entrances and lasting as long as the same actors are on the stage. Study it unit by unit.

The first unit provides the exposition which is designed to put the audience into the picture. In the second unit we see the forward movement of the play as one situation changes into another. The last unit in a tragedy or a tragical play will bring the catastrophe and in comedy — and some of the history plays — an unravelling of the complications, what is called a *dénouement*.

The onward movement of the play from start to finish is its progressive structure. We see the chain of cause and effect (the plot) and the progressive revelation and development of character. The people, their characters and their motives drive the plot forward in a series of scenes which are carefully planned to give variety of pace and excitement. We notice fast-moving and slower-moving episodes, tension mounting and slackening, and alternate fear and hope for the characters we favour. Full-stage scenes, such as stately councils and processions or turbulent mobs, contrast with scenes of small groups or even single speakers. Each of the scenes presents a deed or event which changes the situation. In performances, entrances and exits and stage actions are physical facts, with more impact than on the page. That impact Shakespeare relied upon, and we must restore it by an effort of the imagination.

Shakespeare's language is just as diverse. Quickfire dialogue is followed by long speeches, and verse changes to prose. There is a wide range of speech – formal, colloquial, dialect, 'Mummerset' and the broken English of foreigners, for example. Songs, instrumental music, and the noise of battle, revelry and tempest, all extend the range of dramatic expression. The dramatic use of language is enhanced by skilful stagecraft, by costumes, by properties such as beds, swords and Yorick's skull, by such stage business as kneeling, embracing and giving money, and by use of such features of the stage structure as the balcony and the trapdoor.

By these means Shakespeare's people are brought vividly to life and cleverly individualised. But though they have much to tell us about human nature, we must never forget that they are characters in a play, not in real life. And remember, they exist to enact the play, not the play to portray *them*.

Shakespeare groups his characters so that they form a pattern, and it is useful to draw a diagram showing this. Sometimes a linking character has dealings with each group. The pattern of persons belongs to the symmetric structure of the play, and its dramatic unity is reinforced and enriched by a pattern of resemblances and contrasts; for instance, between characters, scenes, recurrent kinds of imagery, and words. It is not enough just to notice a feature that belongs to the symmetric structure, you should ask what its relevance is to the play as a whole and to the play's ideas.

These ideas and the dramatising of them in a central theme, or several related to each other, are a principal source of the dramatic unity. In order to see what themes are present and important, look, as before, for pattern. Observe the place in it of the leading character. In tragedy this will be the protagonist, in comedy heroes and heroines, together with those in conflict or contrast with them. In *Henry IV Part I*, Prince Hal is being educated for kingship and has a correct estimate of honour, while Falstaff despises honour, and Hotspur makes an idol of it. Pick out the episodes of great intensity as, for example, in *King Lear* where the theme of spiritual blindness is objectified in the blinding of Gloucester, and similarly, note the emphases given by dramatic poetry as in Prospero's 'Our revels now are ended . . .'or unforgettable utterances such as Lear's 'Is there any cause in Nature that makes these hard hearts?' Striking stage-pictures such as that of Hamlet behind the King at prayer will point to leading themes, as will all the parallels and recurrences, including those of phrase and imagery. See whether, in the play you are studying, themes known to be favourites with Shakespeare are prominent, themes such as those of order and disorder, relationships disrupted by mistakes about identity, and appearance and reality. The latter were bound to fascinate Shakespeare, whose theatrical art worked by means of illusions which pointed beyond the surface of actual life to underlying truths. In looking at themes beware of attempts to make the play fit some orthodoxy a critic believes in — Freudian perhaps, or Marxist, or dogmatic Christian theology — and remember that its ideas, though they often have a bearing on ours, are Elizabethan.

Some of Shakespeare's greatness lies in the good parts he wrote for the actors. In his demands upon them, and the opportunities he provided, he bore their professional skills in mind and made use of their physical prowess, relished by a public accustomed to judge fencing and wrestling as expertly as we today judge football and tennis. As a member of the professional group of players called the Chamberlain's Men he knew each actor he was writing for. To play his women he had highly trained boys. As paired heroines they were often contrasted, short with tall, for example, or one vivacious and enterprising, the other more conventionally feminine.

Richard Burbage, the company's leading man, was famous as a great tragic actor, and he took leading roles in seven of Shakespeare's tragedies. Though each of the seven has its own distinctiveness, we shall find at the centre of all of them a tragic protagonist possessing tragic greatness, not just one 'tragic flaw' but a tragic vulnerability. He will have a character which makes him unfit to cope with the tragic situations confronting him, so that his tragic errors bring down upon him tragic suffering and finally a tragic catastrophe. Normally, both the suffering and the catastrophe are far worse than he can be said to deserve, and others are engulfed in them who deserve such a fate less or not at all. Tragic terror is aroused in us because, though exceptional, he is sufficiently near to normal humankind for his fate to remind us of what can happen to human beings like ourselves, and because we see in it a combination of inexorable law and painful mystery. We recognise the principle of cause and effect where in a tragic world errors return upon those who make them, but we are also aware of the tragic disproportion between cause and effect. In a tragic world you may kick a stone and start an avalanche which will destroy you and others with you. Tragic pity is aroused in us by this disproportionate suffering, and also by all the kinds of suffering undergone by every character who has won our imaginative sympathy. Imaginative sympathy is wider than moral approval, and is felt even if suffering does seem a just and logical outcome. In addition to pity and terror we have a sense of tragic waste because catastrophe has affected so much that was great and fine. Yet we feel also a tragic exaltation. To our grief the men and women who represented those values have been destroyed, but the values themselves have been shown not to depend upon success, nor upon immunity from the worst of tragic sufferings and disaster.

Comedies have been of two main kinds, or cross-bred from the two. In critical comedies the governing aim is to bring out the absurdity or irrationality of follies and abuses, and make us laugh at them. Shakespeare's comedies often do this, but most of them belong primarily to the other kind – romantic comedy. Part of the romantic appeal is to our liking for suspense; they are dramas of averted threat, beginning in trouble and ending in joy. They appeal to the romantic senses of adventure and of wonder, and to complain that they are improbable is silly because the improbability, the marvellousness, is part of the pleasure. They dramatise stories of romantic love, accompanied by love doctrine – ideas and ideals of love. But they are plays in two tones, they are comic as well as romantic. There is often something to laugh at even in the love stories of the nobility and gentry, and just as there is high comedy in such incidents as the cross-purposes of the young Athenians in the wood, and Rosalind as 'Ganymede' teasing Orlando, there is always broad comedy for characters of lower rank. Even where one of the sub-plots has no effect on the main plot, it may take up a topic from it and present it in a more comic way.

What is there in the play to make us laugh or smile? We can distinguish many kinds of comedy it may employ. *Language* can amuse by its wit, or by absurdity, as in Bottom's malapropisms. Feste's nonsense-phrases, so fatuously admired by Sir Andrew, are deliberate, while his catechising of Olivia is clown-routine. Ass-headed Bottom embraced by the Fairy Queen is a *comic spectacle* combining costume and stage-business. His wanting to play every part is *comedy of character*. Phebe disdaining Silvius and in love with 'Ganymede', or Malvolio treating Olivia as though she had written him a love-letter is *comedy of situation*; the situation is laughably different from what Phebe or Malvolio supposes. A comic let-down or anticlimax can be devastating, as we see when Aragon, sure that he deserves Portia, chooses the silver casket only to find the portrait not of her but of a 'blinking idiot'. By *slapstick, caricature* or sheer *ridiculousness of situation*, comedy can be exaggerated into farce, which Shakespeare knows how to use on occasion. At the opposite extreme, before he averts the threat, he can carry it to the brink of tragedy, but always under control.

Dramatic irony is the result of a character or the audience anticipating an outcome which, comically or tragically, turns out very differently. Sometimes *we* foresee that it will. The speaker never foresees how ironical, looking back, the words or expectations will appear. When she says, 'A little water clears us of this deed' Lady Macbeth has no prevision of her sleep-walking words, 'Will these hands ne'er be clean?' There is irony in the way in which in all Shakespeare's tragic plays except *Richard II* comedy is found in the very heart of the tragedy. The Porter scene in *Macbeth* comes straight after Duncan's murder. In *Hamlet* and *Antony and Cleopatra* comic episodes lead into the catastrophe: the rustic Countryman brings Cleopatra the means of death, and the satirised Osric departs with Hamlet's assent to the fatal fencing match. The Porter, the Countryman and Osric are not mere 'comic relief'; they contrast with the tragedy in a way that adds something to it, and affects our response.

A sense of the comic and the tragic is common ground between Shakespeare and his audience. Understandings shared with the audience are necessary to all drama. They include conventions, i.e. assumptions, contrary to what factual realism would demand, which the audience silently agrees to accept. It is, after all, by a convention, what Coleridge called a 'willing suspension of disbelief', that an actor is accepted as Hamlet. We should let a play teach us the conventions it depends on. Shakespeare's conventions allow him to take a good many liberties, and he never troubles about inconsistencies that wouldn't trouble an audience. What matters to the dramatist is the effect he creates. So long as we are responding as he would wish, Shakespeare would not care whether we could say by what means he has made us do so. But to appreciate his skill, and get a fuller understanding of his play, we have to distinguish these means, and find terms to describe them.

If you approach the Shakespeare play you are studying bearing in mind what is said to you here, then you will respond to it more fully than before. Yet like all works of artistic genius, Shakespeare's can only be analysed so far. His drama and its poetry will always have about them something 'which into words no critic can digest'.

HAROLD BROOKS

1 LIFE AND BACKGROUND

1.1 LIFE

William Shakespeare was born in 1564 in Stratford upon Avon, a small market town in the West Midlands. His father, John Shakespeare, came from a family of yeomen (independent farmers) a few miles outside Stratford, but John moved into the town and became a tradesman, eventually owning his own shop. He prospered, bought property, and held various civic offices, including that of Bailiff, the chief civic dignitary of Stratford. There is no record of William's schooling, but there can be little doubt that, as the son of a prosperous citizen, he went to Stratford Grammar School, which was free for the sons of Stratford burgesses. In 1582 he married Anne Hathaway, the daughter of a Stratford yeoman, by whom he had three children.

Apart from the dates of his christening, his marriage and the births of his children, we have no firm knowledge of Shakespeare's life until 1592, when the London pamphleteer and dramatist Robert Greene attacked him as an 'upstart crow'; the burden of the attack is that a mere actor should have the presumption to write plays in competition with educated men like Greene. From this attack it is clear that Shakespeare was in London and was already a dramatist of some reputation. His earliest plays date from around 1590, and he probably went to London and became an actor there not long before that date. For, unlike Greene and his friends (university men who wrote for the theatre from outside), Shakespeare was an actor and a professional man of the theatre, and his prosperity rested on the success of the theatrical company he belonged to. No doubt his plays were a great asset for his troupe, but it was his position as a 'sharer' in the outstanding theatrical company of the age which made him a man of substance.

London theatrical companies were co-operative ventures: a number of actors (the sharers) put down the money to buy the necessary equipment (books, properties), hired a theatre, and shared the takings after each performance. The sharers did the bulk of the acting themselves, but they could also hire journeymen actors by the day or the week, and for the women's parts they had boys,who had the status of apprentices; there were no professional actresses in Shakespeare's time. For legal reasons each company had a patron, usually some great nobleman, whose name it took; but in fact the companies were independent commercial organizations.

In 1594, Shakespeare and seven other actors formed a new theatrical company, the Lord Chamberlain's Men. When King James I came to the throne in 1603, he took the company under his own patronage, and changed its name to the King's Men. Besides being extremely successful with the London public, the company was often invited to perform at court before the sovereign during the Christmas revels and similar festivities, and Shakespeare's plays were frequently performed on such occasions.

For, as in the 1590s the Chamberlain's Men established themselves as London's leading company, so Shakespeare established himself as its pre-eminent playwright. His career as a dramatist lasted about twenty years, and for most of this period he wrote about two plays per year. In the early part of his career these were mainly history plays and comedies, but from 1600 onwards he wrote mainly tragedies and 'problem plays', until the very end of his career, when he wrote the so-called romances. In about 1612 he retired from the London theatre and went back to Stratford, where his wife and children had continued to live and where he now owned one of the finest houses in the town. He died in 1616.

1.2 THE HISTORICAL BACKGROUND

During Shakespeare's lifetime there was a period of relative stability and peace in English society. This period of calm occurred between two periods of tumult and change, the Reformation and the Civil Wars. The Reformation was the breaking away of the English church from the authority of the Pope in Rome, and was initiated by Henry VIII about twenty-five years before Shakespeare was born. There followed a period of conflict between Protestants (reformers) and Catholics (traditionalists), erupting at times into armed rebellion, both under Edward VI (a Protestant) and under Queen Mary (a Catholic). In the early part of her reign, Queen Elizabeth I (1558-1603) also had to contend with armed insurrection, like the

Rising of the Northern Earls (1569); but this was the last serious rebellion of her reign, and for the rest of the century England was relatively tranquil. There were still tensions below the surface, however, and these intensified during the seventeenth century, until, twenty-five years after Shakespeare's death, England was plunged into the Civil Wars (1640-49), the armed struggle between King and Parliament which can well be called the English Revolution.

The Reformation and the Civil Wars were major stages in the change from feudal England to capitalist England. In Shakespeare's lifetime, English society still had feudal forms and a feudal social structure, but these were under increasing pressure from within: from Puritans, who wished to carry the Reformation further and to abolish bishops; from scientists, who were undermining traditional views of the universe; from capitalist landlords and merchants who, especially in south-eastern England, were trying to evade traditional controls on economic activity.

The age of Shakespeare, then, was one both of stability and of tension, and both the stability and the tension were important for his art. The period of relative calm and prosperity in the second half of Elizabeth's reign provided material conditions in which a professional English theatre could flourish: the social tensions provided, if only indirectly, the subject-matter for the greatest plays of this theatre.

1.3 THE SOCIAL HIERARCHY

In Elizabethan society there was a well-defined hierarchy, in other words a series of graded ranks. In theory, every individual belonged to one of these grades, and so had a clearly defined social status. Four main grades were recognised: (i) gentlemen, (ii) citizens (masters of a trade), (iii) yeomen (independent farmers), and (iv) artificers and labourers. The reality of Elizabethan society was a good deal more complicated than this, but the theory shows the kind of attitude to the social order which was normal at the time.

The top social group, that of the gentlemen, was subdivided into a large number of graded ranks. At the top was the prince (or sovereign); then came the peers or nobility (dukes, marquises, earls, viscounts, barons); and finally the lesser gentry (knights, esquires, gentlemen). It will be noticed that in Shakespeare's time the word *gentleman* had two different meanings: it could refer to the whole of the top group of society, including knights, noblemen, and even the monarch; but it was also used of one sub-group of this class, namely the lowest, the simple gentleman. In *Richard II*, Mowbray, who is a duke, undertakes to prove himself 'a loyal gentleman' (I.i.148), and Bolingbroke refers to King Richard himself as 'A happy gentleman in blood and lineaments' (III.i.9). On the other hand, when York says that he has dispatched one of his gentlemen with a message to the Queen (III.i.40), he is probably using the word in its narrower sense.

In Shakespeare's England, the gentlemen (in the wide sense) probably represented only about 5 per cent of the population, but they had almost all the power, and many privileges. In Shakespeare's plays, the central characters are nearly always gentlemen (or ladies), but there are also many characters from other social groups — citizens, foresters, grave-diggers, inn-keepers, porters, ordinary sailors, tailors, waiting-women, watchmen, yeomen, and so on. In *Richard II,* however, it is striking that such non-gentle characters are almost entirely absent from the play. The two central characters, Richard and Bolingbroke, are members of the royal family, as also are Gaunt, York, Aumerle, and the three main women in the play; most of the other characters are members of the nobility, though there are also a few knights (like Bushy and Bagot). Non-gentle characters may fill out the scene as attendants, officers, soldiers, and so on, but rarely have speaking parts. There are indeed the gardeners in III.iv, but these are not presented realistically, and are highly emblematic figures. The only other non-gentle character to speak more than a few words is the groom in V.v, and the play as a whole moves in a rarefied upper-class atmosphere, uninterrupted by common accents or the common touch.

In Elizabethan England, as in many hierarchical societies, there were clear ways of marking social distinctions — by clothes, by modes of address, by ceremonies of respect. For centuries there had been laws regulating the kinds of clothes permitted for different social groups, and on the Elizabethan stage it would be immediately apparent from their dress that some characters were, for example, noblemen and others artisans or servants. People were also careful to use correct modes of address, such as 'my lord', 'sir', 'your grace', 'madam', and so on, making explicit the status of the person addressed. In *Richard II,* York reproaches Northumberland for referring to the king as 'Richard', instead of 'King Richard' (III.iii.6-8); Northumberland's disregard of the correct form at this point is of course a sign of Richard's fall. As for ceremonies of respect, it was obligatory for a man to remove his hat in the presence of somebody of much higher rank (and Elizabethan men usually wore hats all the time, both indoors and out). A more extreme mark of respect was kneeling, especially in supplication or in submission.

Such ceremonies of respect are exceptionally frequent in *Richard II,* and play a large part in the visual effect of a performance.

1.4 THE MONARCH

At the top of the social hierarchy was the monarch (prince, sovereign). There was a commonly held view, known as the Divine Right of Kings, that monarchs derived their authority directly from God. A legitimate monarch was God's deputy on earth, responsible to God alone, and not to his subjects. Rebellion against the monarch was therefore a rebellion against God, and a sin. There could obviously be the problem, in particular cases, of deciding whether or not a ruler was a legitimate one. In Shakespeare's *Richard III,* rebellion against a king is depicted as virtuous, since the king is a tyrant and usurper. In *Richard II,* arguments for and against Bolingbroke's rebellion are presented by various characters, and the audience left to judge.

Although the doctrine of Divine Right was widespread in Europe, it was not unchallenged. In the Middle Ages, the doctrine had often been used to support the Emperor against the Pope. Many Catholic theorists, consequently, denied the doctrine of Divine Right, and claimed that the Church was superior to the state, and that the Pope had the power to excommunicate kings and release their subjects from their allegiance. Indeed, in 1570 Pope Pius V excommunicated Queen Elizabeth I, and the Catholic Church incited her subjects to rebel against her. A different challenge to Divine Right theory came from the rise of secular theories of government, in other words theories which were not grounded in religion. Such were the political theories of Niccolo Machiavelli, whose ideas gradually spread through Europe during the sixteenth century.

The theory of Divine Right, therefore, though commonly held in Elizabethan England (and certainly held by Queen Elizabeth I herself), was not the only possible view. Moreover, the doctrine of Divine Right does not necessarily imply that the monarch has unlimited power. In the Middle Ages, supporters of Divine Right did not argue for the absolute power of kings; this was an argument which arose in the sixteenth century, especially in France. In England, the view that the power of kings is absolute did not become common until the seventeenth century, when the conflict between King and Parliament became intense.

So in the Elizabethan public theatre of the 1590s, when *Richard II* was first performed, many of the audience (but not all) would probably have accepted the Divine Right view; but few of them would have been likely to believe that a monarch has absolute power, unlimited by the law and custom of the land.

1.5 THE WORLD-PICTURE

The Divine Right theory was part of a set of beliefs widely held in Elizabethan England. These beliefs reflect the hierarchical forms of Elizabethan society, and the idea of order or hierarchy is central. The whole universe formed one vast hierarchy, from God down to the minerals; there were no gaps in the chain, and everything had a place in it. Below God were the angels, arranged in nine ranks; then came human beings, arranged in social classes; then three grades of animal life; then vegetable life; and finally, at the bottom of the pyramid, inanimate objects. The world was made of four elements (earth, air, fire, water), each of which was composed of a pair of four fundamental qualities (hot, cold, moist, dry). The elements were arranged hierarchically: at the top was fire, the region of meteors, then came air, then water (the oceans), and at the bottom (the dregs of the universe) was earth. But the heavens, from the sphere of the moon upwards, were not composed of the four elements, but of a fifth element, the quintessence or ether, which was perfect and unchanging.

In the Great Chain of Being, stretching from God down to the minerals, Man was located at a critical point, providing the link between matter and spirit. Moreover, he constituted a kind of miniature universe (or microcosm), for there were detailed resemblances between his body and the universe. For example, just as the universe was believed to be made of the four elements, so a man's temperament was thought to be determined by the balance within him of four fluids, called humours, composed of pairs of the same four qualities: melancholy was cold and dry (like earth), phlegm cold and moist (like water), blood warm and moist (like air), and choler warm and dry (like fire). The four elements and the four humours play a dominant part in the imagery of *Richard II*.

The hierarchies within the universe were similar to one another in various ways: as God was head of the universe, so the king was head of society, the lion was the king of beasts, the eagle the king of birds, the sun the chief of the heavenly bodies, the head the chief part of the human body, and so on. The equating of the king with the sun, the eagle, the lion, and even with God is found in *Richard II*.

According to this world view, it is natural for people to accept their place in the social hierarchy: it is natural (and therefore right) for subjects to obey their king, for women to obey their husbands, for children to obey their parents. In practice, of course, people were not always obedient, and there were groups in society which were opposed to established authority. So the insistence of the government on the sinfulness of disobedience was not merely a reflection of the social hierarchy, but also an attempt to maintain it. Tudor governments took great pains to inculcate obedience and acquiescence in one's social station, for example by means of official sermons on obedience read in all churches.

1.6 THE SPIRIT OF THE 1590s

In the 1590s, the decade in which Shakespeare began his career as a dramatist, there was a strong sense of national unity and of patriotism. Queen Elizabeth I, faced with contending social forces (especially Catholics versus Puritans) had pursued a policy of compromise and social conciliation. In her church settlement, she tried to make the Church of England acceptable to as many people as possible: the monarch was head of the church, and it was governed by bishops, thus maintaining the forms of a hierarchical society; but many disputed points of doctrine were deliberately left ambiguous, and from most of the population Elizabeth required only an outward conformity, saying that she had no 'windows on men's souls'.

In the 1580s, after some years of relative tranquillity, there was a growing sense of national unity and national pride. These feelings were greatly encouraged by the events of 1588, when Spain, the most powerful of the Catholic countries, attempted to invade England with the so-called Great Armada. The Armada was crushingly defeated; but, what was even more important, the expected Catholic revolt in England did not take place. Nobody knew how many secret Catholics there were in England, nor how many of them belonged to the militant wing which advocated armed rebellion; but when the Armada sailed up the Channel, many people certainly hoped for or feared a major Catholic rising. But in the event, the expected Catholic rebellion just did not materialise, and the exhilaration and sense of national unity in the years after 1588 were surely due to this fact as much as to the defeat of the Armada.

Even so, there were still anxieties. The Queen was growing old, and had no heir, and people were concerned about the succession. Moreover, now that the fear of a Catholic counter-revolution had disappeared, puritans and parliamentarians felt less need to support the Crown, and opposition to the government became more vocal. So beneath the surface unity and the national ardour there were still social tensions, though these did not become severe until the reign of James I.

It will be seen that Shakespeare's career as a dramatist came at a critical point in English history. The first decade of his writing occurred in the upsurge of national confidence and exhilaration which followed the defeat of the Armada. In the theatre, these feelings are reflected in the great popularity of history plays and romantic comedies. The history plays tend to handle the events of England's past in a patriotic manner; they are a common theatrical type until about 1605, after which time they almost entirely disappear. Shakespeare's romantic comedies can be seen as celebrations of the English community in his time, in all its variety and robustness. But from about 1600, as England begins to move into a period of social crisis and conflict, Shakespeare's work shows a marked change: there are no more history plays or romantic comedies, and instead there are tragedies and problem plays, which explore the growing social crisis of the age, not directly, but through ideas, attitudes, conflicting world-views.

1.7 SHAKESPEARE'S HISTORY PLAYS

(a) The History Cycle

By history plays, we mean ones dealing with *English* history. Shakespeare wrote ten of them, and with one exception they were all written in the 1590s. The exception is *Henry VIII*, written in collaboration with John Fletcher right at the end of Shakespeare's career. Of the nine plays from the 1590s, *King John* stands by itself. The remaining eight plays depict one continuous period of English history from the reign of Richard II in the fourteenth century to the accession of Henry VII, the first of the Tudor Kings, in 1485. These eight plays are often called Shakespeare's history cycle.

The cycle falls into two groups of four plays each, often referred to as the two tetralogies, and the plays depicting the earlier historical events in fact form the group of plays which was written second. *Richard II* (c. 1595) depicts the deposition and murder of Richard II by his cousin Henry Bolingbroke, Duke of Lancaster, who becomes king as Henry IV. The two parts of *Henry IV* (c. 1597) show the civil disturbances of Henry's reign, a consequence of his seizure of the crown, as the noblemen who had helped him to the throne rebel against him in turn. In *Henry V,* the troubles of the Lancastrian monarchy are temporarily smoothed over, as Henry IV's son, the warrior-king Henry V, leads his English army to the conquest of

France. But retribution for the Lancastrian usurpation of the crown is merely postponed: in the other half of the cycle, the consequences of the original murder and deposition of Richard II come home to roost. The three parts of *Henry VI* (c. 1590-91) show how, after the death of Henry V, the English possessions in France are lost, and then civil war breaks out in England (the Wars of the Roses), as the Duke of York challenges the Lancastrian right to the throne. After bloody wars and murders, the Yorkists triumph, and the eldest son of the Duke of York becomes king as Edward IV. In *Richard III* (c. 1593) the youngest brother of Edward IV schemes and murders his way to the throne, and becomes Richard III, but finally this monster-king is overthrown and killed by Henry Tudor, Earl of Richmond, who unites the houses of York and Lancaster by marrying the Yorkist heiress, and inaugurates the Tudor era as Henry VII.

(b) Was the cycle planned?
This account of the history cycle seems to assume that all eight plays were planned from the start as a single unit. In fact it is extremely doubtful whether, when Shakespeare wrote the first four plays, he already had in mind the writing of the other four. On the other hand, the eight plays do hang together extremely well, and give a largely consistent interpretation of nearly a hundred years of English history.

Moreover, the four plays initiated by *Richard II* (often referred to collectively as the *Henriad)* do look as though they were planned as a single unit. In the two *Henry IV* plays, characters are constantly harking back to the events depicted in *Richard II*, and using them as an explanation or justification for their present actions. This does not of course prove that Shakespeare had already foreseen such links when he was writing *Richard II*; but in fact there are features in *Richard II* itself which prepare the way for the later plays, and suggest that Shakespeare already envisaged the *Henry IV* plays. For example, Shakespeare sets up the contrast and conflict between Harry Percy and Prince Hal which is to form a central theme in *Henry IV Part I*: at the beginning of Act V scene iii of *Richard II* Bolingbroke (now Henry IV) laments the wildness of his eldest son, and Harry Percy tells of a meeting he has had with the prince; this little passage of 20 lines has little to do with the themes of *Richard II,* but does point forward clearly to the next play in the sequence. Moreover, in order to set up the opposition between Harry Percy (Hotspur) and Prince Hal, Shakespeare had to bend the facts of history: the historical Harry Percy was a generation older than Prince Hal (and in fact two years older than Bolingbroke), but Shakespeare made him a young man about the same age as Hal; moreover, this change of age has already taken place in *Richard II* (see II.iii.41-4), which suggests that Shakespeare was already planning the layout of *Henry IV Part I.*

The civil wars which are to follow the Lancastrian usurpation are also prefigured in *Richard II*: the Bishop of Carlisle's long speech denouncing Bolingbroke and prophesying civil war (IV.i.114-49) is more than once recalled later in the *Henriad;* and Richard's speech to Northumberland prophesying future conflict between the Percies and Bolingbroke (V.i.55-68) is actually quoted by Bolingbroke in *Henry IV Part 2* (III.i.70-9).

These, and a few other thematic links, suggest that Shakespeare planned the *Henriad* as a single unit. Some critics, however, disagree: M.C. Bradbrook, for example, is sceptical about the theory, and in particular inclines to the view that *Henry IV Part 2* was an afterthought, a hastily written encore: and she argues that the Henry IV plays and *Henry V* are about human relationships and heroic acts, not about politics.

(c) Straddling two ages

The plays of the History Cycle are both about the late Middle Ages and about Shakespeare's own age. They depict the breakdown of medieval society and the coming of the Tudors, but at the same time offer frequent parallels to sixteenth-century England. For example, there are implicit parallels between the Lancastrian kings (Henry IV and Henry V) and the Tudors. These comparisons tend to be kept below the surface, however, and the general effect of the Cycle is to reinforce the Tudor view of history. For when Henry VII came to the throne, he took great pains to get the history of the preceding events written from the Tudor point of view, and to suppress evidence that contradicted it. Hence Shakespeare and his contemporaries inherited a set of history-books in which rebellion was a moral and political evil; in which Richard III was a monster, while Henry VII had a good lineal title to the throne (neither true); and which showed how a period of civil war, caused by usurpation, was brought to an end by a saintly Henry Tudor, who united the families of York and Lancaster and restored peace and prosperity to England. This was the general historical framework in which, inevitably, Shakespeare had to work.

(d) Richard II and Elizabeth I

In the case of *Richard II,* however, there was a different topical parallel, and a potentially dangerous one. In the 1580s and 1590s, comparisons were often made between Richard II and Elizabeth I: both were childless, and so lacking a direct heir; and malcontents argued that, like Richard, Elizabeth was surrounded by bad counsellors. Since Richard II was one of the few English kings to have been deposed, and his case was frequently discussed in works dealing with the problems of usurpation and deposition, the linking of his name with Elizabeth's inevitably carried hints of deposition. In 1601, the day before the rash and disastrous rebellion of the Earl of Essex, some of the Earl's followers paid the Lord Chamberlain's Men (Shakespeare's company) to put on at the Globe a performance of a play about the deposing and killing of Richard II, presumably to encourage the idea that a monarch could be made to abdicate. It is likely (though not certain) that this was Shakespeare's play. After the rebellion, members of the company were questioned by the authorities. Later in 1601, Elizabeth herself is reported to have said, 'I am Richard II, know ye not that?'.

The subject of the play, therefore, was politically sensitive. This is reflected in the fact that the deposition scene (IV.i.154-318) is missing from the early printed editions of the play, presumably because of censorship. There were three editions of the play in Elizabeth's reign, in 1597, 1598, and 1598 again, and in none of these does the deposition scene appear. It first appeared in the fourth edition of 1608, when Elizabeth was safely dead. It is not known whether, during Elizabeth's reign, the deposition scene was performed on the stage, even though removed from the printed texts; but it is probable that it was.

2 SUMMARY AND
CRITICAL COMMENTARY

2.1 NOTE

The earliest printed editions of *Richard II* regularly use the spelling *Bullingbrook* or *Bullingbrooke,* which many modern editions change to *Bolingbroke*: and they frequently use the spelling *Herford* instead of *Hereford.* I shall use the forms *Bolingbroke* and *Hereford,* since these are the ones you are most likely to meet in modern editions and in critical works. (Notice however the rhyme 'look/Bolingbroke' at III.iv.98-9.) Line-references are from *Richard II,* edited by Richard Adams (Macmillan Education, 1975), in the Macmillan Shakespeare series. Since, however, the play is entirely in verse, line-references vary very little from one modern edition to another. For other Shakespeare plays, line-references are taken from *The Riverside Shakespeare,* edited by G. Blakemore Evans (Houghton Mifflin, Boston, 1974).

2.2 GENERAL SUMMARY

King Richard II banishes his cousin, Henry Bolingbroke, for six years, after Bolingbroke has been involved in a furious political dispute about a murder in which the King himself has in fact been implicated. On his death-bed, Bolingbroke's father, John of Gaunt, Duke of Lancaster, reproaches the King his nephew for his misrule, but to no effect. After Gaunt's death, the King seizes his estates, which he uses to finance a military expedition to Ireland. While the King is in Ireland, Bolingbroke returns to England with an army, saying that his sole aim is to claim his inheritance as Duke of Lancaster; he is joined by many noblemen who are discontented with the misrule of Richard and his favourites. Richard is detained in

Ireland by unfavourable winds, and when he finally lands in Wales support for him has melted away. He asserts his God-given right to the crown, but in the face of Bolingbroke's military power his moral resistance collapses, and he virtually offers to surrender the throne to Bolingbroke. Bolingbroke takes Richard to London as a prisoner. In Parliament, Richard formally abdicates in favour of Bolingbroke, who ascends the throne as King Henry IV. Richard is imprisoned at Pomfret Castle, and is murdered there at the King's instigation. Henry, however, refuses to reward the murderer, and follows Richard's funeral bier, declaring his intention of undertaking a pilgrimage to the Holy Land to expiate his guilt.

2.3 SCENE BY SCENE SUMMARY AND CRITICAL COMMENTARY

Act I, Scene i

Summary
The action of the play opens in April 1398. Henry Bolingbroke, Duke of Hereford, a cousin to the King, and Thomas Mowbray, Duke of Norfolk, appear before King Richard II and formally accuse one another of treason. They challenge each other to judicial combat to prove their accusations. The most serious charge is that Mowbray was responsible for the murder of Thomas of Woodstock, Duke of Gloucester, an uncle of the King, which he denies. The King and John of Gaunt, Duke of Lancaster, father of Bolingbroke, try to reconcile the disputants, but without success. The King orders them to meet in judicial combat at Coventry on 17 September.

Commentary
The scene at once offers the splendour, spectacle and formality which are characteristic of the play. King Richard takes the centre of the stage, surrounded by his court. Since he is about to exercise his judicial function as the highest judge in the country, he presumably takes his seat on his throne, the 'state' which often occupied the back centre of the stage in an Elizabethan theatre. The throne probably stood on a high dais, so that the king was decidedly higher than his subjects. The two antagonists, Mowbray and Bolingbroke, are now brought in, one on each side of the stage, and hurl their accusations at

each other across the front of the king and his court. At lines 158-9 there is a movement outwards from the centre, when Gaunt goes to his son and Richard to Mowbray to try to calm them. When this fails, Richard moves across to Bolingbroke to try to persuade him. This too fails, and Richard moves back to the centre to give his judgement, for which he would resume his seat on the throne. The scene is therefore largely static as spectacle: apart from the moves outward of Gaunt and Richard, the only actions are ritualistic – the throwing down of gages, Mowbray's kneeling to the king.

The language of the play, too, at once strikes a note of formal ceremony. Richard's enquiries of Gaunt in the opening lines are measured, formal and king-like, and Gaunt's replies are equally weighty and decorous (even though he is implicitly taking the side of his son). The audience is given the impression of a court which is well-ordered and ruled by forms, and this impression is reinforced by the lines spoken by Richard while the antagonists are being summoned (15-19), with their strong verbal patterning and their neat concluding rhyme. Mowbray and Bolingbroke exchange their accusations and counter-accusations in a magnificent high style (mainly blank verse, but with occasional rhymes); it is sometimes said that the poetry of the play is lyrical, but these passages are far from lyrical: rather they are heroic in style, and often splendidly so, as in Mowbray's lines about the frozen ridges of the Alps (62–6). The passions expressed are violent, but they are held in restraint by a style which is decorous and formal. This sense of control is reinforced by the use of rhyming couplets, especially at the ends of speeches or passages, and by the ritual nature of the actions (Mowbray and Bolingbroke do not spit at each other, but throw down gages).

During all this, Richard plays the part of the impartial arbitrator, and clearly knows what it is proper for him to say, as when he assures the opponents that Bolingbroke's kinship to him will not sway his judgement (115–23). His antipathy to Bolingbroke does perhaps show through when he expresses mild surprise at the idea that Mowbray may have committed something heinous (84–6); but his tone throughout is judicious and calm.

Bolingbroke makes three accusations against Mowbray (87–108): (1) that he had misappropriated a sum of money due to the king; (2) that all the treasonous plots in England during the past eighteen years had been initiated by him; and (3) that he had been responsible for the murder of the Duke of Gloucester. Mowbray answers the first accusation by accounting for the money; the second is largely rhetorical, and Mowbray not unreasonably dismisses it as the product of 'rancour' (143); it is the third accusation, the murder of

Gloucester, which is the crucial one, as everyone on stage well knows. Mowbray's answer to it is curiously ambiguous:

> I slew him not, but to mine own disgrace
> Neglected my sworn duty in that case.
> (133–4)

This might mean that Mowbray had failed to kill Gloucester, even though it had been his duty to do so; or that he had failed in his duty to protect Gloucester from murder (since Gloucester was in his custody at the time). How much is the audience expected to know about these events? Some critics take the view that the original audience would have known that Mowbray had instigated the murder on Richard's instructions. This seems a somewhat dangerous assumption. It looks rather as though Shakespeare at this stage is deliberately leaving the matter open, and that the ambiguity of Mowbray's reply is quite calculated. Who is telling the truth? Everything is left in doubt. Later in the play (IV.i.1–106) Bolingbroke tries to get to the truth of the matter, and he too is left with uncertainties and contradictory stories. This indeed is one of the themes of the whole play — the uncertain relationship between language and reality, the gap between the tongue and the event.

On this view, the audience does not know at this stage that Richard himself is implicated in Gloucester's murder (though they will learn in the next scene). So in Scene i Richard appears as an even–handed and competent king, and as yet there are no hints of murder or of misrule. Yet Richard's implication in the murder plainly affects his behaviour. He makes no attempt whatever to probe the truth or otherwise of Bolingbroke's accusations. Instead, he treats the whole thing as a personal quarrel between Mowbray and Bolingbroke, and tries to reconcile them (152–95): his 'Forget, forgive' is completely conventional, and made to sound even more banal by the end-stopped rhyming couplets; while his joke about blood-letting is urbane but not very amusing. When this appeal fails he tries to assert his authority (164, 173–4, 186), but this too has no effect, since both Mowbray and Bolingbroke stand on their honour, the reputation they would lose by retraction or reconciliation. Finally, he gives a clear and decisive judgement, setting a day for the judicial combat (198–205). Even so, a basic weakness has been exposed: he asserts his position and his authority, but cannot make it good. Lions make leopards tame, he says: but he cannot tame either Mowbray or Bolingbroke. And his sweeping assertion of his hereditary power –

16

'We were not born to sue but to command' – is immediately followed by the tame confession 'Which since we cannot do . . .' (196–7).

The scene introduces a good deal of the complex web of imagery which is to dominate the play. The major word is *blood,* which occurs in various meanings: it can be used in its literal sense, whether it is let by a physician to effect a cure (153), shed in combat (149, 172), or shed in murder (103–104); it can refer to the passions (high mettle, anger) believed to result from hot blood or excess of blood (51); and it can mean 'lineage, descent, kindred, blood relationship' (58, 71, 113, 119). Blood relationship and the shedding of blood meet in the story of Cain, who killed his brother Abel (104), a reference to be picked up again at the end of the play. Blood is one of the four humours, and another, choler, is also mentioned (153); and the four elements also occur throughout the scene in various guises, for example: sea (19), fire (19), earth (23, 37, 105), clouds (42), land (96), loam (179), clay (179). The land (96) is England, and both the earth in general and England in particular play a large part in the imagery of the play. The scene also introduces the theme of language and the truth: flattery (25), the tongue as the organ of speech (49, 190). Linked to this is the frequent use of titles, often long and cere-monious: the very first line of the play is 'Old John of Gaunt, time-honoured Lancaster', a line which also shows Richard's cons-ciousness of the gap between his own generation and Gaunt's.

The scene, then, introduces many of the themes and image–clusters which will dominate the play. It shows Richard in confident command of a formal and ceremonious court, but hints at his weakness and also depicts the violent passions (in Mowbray and Bolingbroke) which threaten its order. It depicts Bolingbroke as a man of fiery courage and high aspiration (note especially Richard's comment at line 109); while Gaunt by contrast is established as an elder statesman and peacemaker. Later in the play (IV.i.1–106) there is a parallel scene, in which it is Bolingbroke instead of Richard who holds the centre of the stage and acts as the impartial judge.

Act 1, Scene ii

Summary
Gaunt converses with the Duchess of Gloucester, widow of the murdered duke. The Duchess incites him to take revenge for the murder. Gaunt refuses: the responsibility for the murder rests with God's anointed deputy (the King), and it must be left to God to take revenge. They part, he to go to Coventry to see the combat between

Bolingbroke and Mowbray, she to her country house to mourn and to die.

Commentary

After the colourful spectacle of the opening scene, Shakespeare gives us a sombre second scene. There are only two characters, a widow (who would be dressed in black) and an elder statesman (who would also be quietly attired, at any rate compared to the young men of the court). The subject matter, too, is sombre – murder, revenge, Christian patience. After the extravagant rhetorical accusations of the first scene, Scene ii is relatively low key, despite the Duchess's vehemence: having got the audience emotionally involved in Scene i, the dramatist can now afford to lower the emotional temperature and offer us a scene which develops themes and gives information.

The most important piece of information given to the audience is that Richard himself had been responsible for the murder of Gloucester. This is stated quite explicitly by Gaunt (4–5, 37–41), and we have no reason to disbelieve him. He does not mean that the King personally killed Gloucester, but that 'the butchers of his life' (3) had acted on the King's instructions. Among the murderers the Duchess specifically names 'butcher Mowbray' (48), but Gaunt does not confirm or comment on this, and the question of Mowbray's implication is left open throughout the play.

The scene also introduces two different attitudes to one of the central political questions of the play – What action should be taken when a legitimate monarch behaves unjustly? Gaunt preaches patience: his view is the orthodox one which regards the King as God's anointed deputy on earth, against whom rebellion is a sin; revenge must be left to God (37–41). The Duchess argues for action: Gaunt's patience, she says, is really despair, and his passivity is an invitation (to the King, it is implied) to murder him too (29–36).

The scene also develops the imagery introduced in the first scene. Blood is again central: it is the kinship between Gaunt and Gloucester (1, 12, 17, 22), it is the blood shed in Gloucester's murder (21), it is the passion and vengefulness which Gaunt lacks (because his blood lacks fire) (10). The seven sons of King Edward III (of whom Richard's father, the Black Prince, was the eldest, John of Gaunt the fourth, Edmund Langley, Duke of York the fifth, and Thomas Woodstock Duke of Gloucester the youngest) are seven vials of Edward's sacred blood (11–12). But to this image is added that of the tree, with its root, its summer leaves, and its seven branches (13–20); the root links it to the earth imagery of the play, the branches to the theme of generation and blood relationship, and the leaves to the imagery of vegetation, and especially of gardens, which permeates the play. The element of fire appears (10), and the element of water in the form of the Duchess's tears (74); tears occur frequently in the play.

Act 1, Scene iii

Summary
Bolingbroke and Mowbray appear fully armed in the lists at Coventry before the King and his court for the judicial combat. They take a ceremonious farewell of their friends and of the King. The signal is given for the combat to begin, but at the last moment Richard throws down his staff into the lists to stop the proceedings. After a consultation with his council, he summons the combatants before him, and sentences them both to exile. Bolingbroke is exiled for ten years and Mowbray for life. After Mowbray's departure, Richard reduces Bolingbroke's sentence to six years. Gaunt tries, with little success, to reconcile his son to six years of exile.

Commentary
In this scene we return to the colourful spectacle and the pomp and ceremony of the opening scene. At line 6 the trumpets sound and there is a ceremonial entry by Richard and his court. Richard would again take his seat on the throne back centre, and the two combatants, when summoned, would occupy opposite sides of the stage. The preliminaries of the combat (1–117) are highly ritualistic, with trumpets sounding, the formal questioning of the champions by the Lord Marshal, the giving of the lances, heralds uttering the challenge and the acceptance of it, and the use of long rolling titles, notably 'Harry of Hereford, Lancaster, and Derby' (35, 100, 104). Even when the combatants hold up the proceedings in order to take their farewells of the King and of their friends, it is a 'ceremonious leave' that they take (50). In these farewell speeches both Bolingbroke and Mowbray strike a note of elation and of delight in action. Bolingbroke is as confident as a falcon (61), and is 'lusty, young, and cheerly drawing breath' (66); Mowbray's 'dancing soul' celebrates this 'feast of battle' (91–2).

This impending 'battle' is a judicial combat, which is not to be confused with either a duel or a tournament. The judicial combat, or Trial by Battle, had been introduced into English law at the Norman Conquest, and was not formally abolished until the nineteenth century, though in effect it had fallen into disuse by Shakespeare's day. It was a completely official legal method of settling certain types of dispute, and it was believed that God gave the victory to the combatant who had justice on his side. The duel, by contrast, was a private fight, in which rapiers were used, and was illegal; it was only just coming into England from the Continent in Shakespeare's youth. Defenders of the duel often claimed that it was a form of judicial combat, but its status was in fact quite different. The tournament, on the other hand, was a kind of sporting and social event, although, since it was a form of mimic battle, there were occasional fatalities; it persisted in England until about 1600, and Shakespeare may have drawn on the ceremonies of Elizabethan tournaments for his depiction of the Trial by Battle.

By line 117, then, the audience is keyed up to witness a judicial combat. The combatants have perhaps gone off-stage, one each side, to mount their horses (for it was not practicable to bring horses on to the Elizabethan stage). The trumpets sound a charge, and the Lord Marshal gives the word for the battle to begin. But then comes anticlimax. Richard throws down his warder to stop the combat, and there is a long flourish on the trumpets while he consults his advisers, and the two combatants remove their helmets and return to their chairs. So there is no fighting after all, and this is typical of the whole play: people strike attitudes, utter threats, raise military forces, but never in fact fight. Actions in the play, as the critic Tillyard says, tend to be symbolic rather than real.

In historical fact, Richard's consultation with his council went on for 'two long hours', during which time Bolingbroke and Mowbray had to sit in their chairs and wait. Shakespeare's compression of this period into a matter of seconds is an obvious dramatic necessity, but is perhaps also meant to suggest that Richard had already decided on his course of action before the combat, and that the consultation was a mere formality. The sentences on Bolingbroke and Mowbray are in fact a skilful political manoeuvre which gets Richard out of a difficult situation and leaves him in a position of considerable strength. He has prevented the combat, in which a victory for Bolingbroke would have been generally interpreted as a judgement by God; he has got rid of a powerful and ambitious political opponent; and he has also got rid of a potentially inconvenient ally.

From Mowbray's reproachful reaction to the sentence (154–173) it is clear that he feels that Richard has let him down and is treating him unjustly. The lines are remarkable for their concentration on speech and the speech-organs: Mowbray's lament is that he will be forced to live among people who do not understand English so that exile will be 'speechless death'. Richard's curt dismissal of his complaint

(174–175) is callous: he has jettisoned Mowbray, apparently without compunction.

When Richard reduces Bolingbroke's exile by four years, it is the power of a king's word which strikes the latter; there is a hint of both envy and ambition in his comment (213–15). Gaunt, by contrast, comments on the limitations of a king's power (226–32), which cannot affect human mortality; implicit here is the contrast between Man and Office which is to be developed later. Richard reminds Gaunt that Gaunt himself had participated in the decision to exile his son (233–5); whereupon Gaunt makes explicit the theme of speech and thought, and the gap between them (236–46): when his tongue agreed to the verdict, it had not truly reflected his thoughts and feelings.

Richard and his court make a ceremonious exit, and Bolingbroke is left to bid his father farewell. Here again we have the contrast between words and thoughts: we know that the advice and the consolations which Gaunt offers to his son do not reflect what he really feels about his exile; and Bolingbroke himself says that he cannot find sufficient words to express his grief (255–7).The exchanges between father and son are extremely conventional, beginning with a passage of stichomythia (dialogue in alternate lines) using antithesis and obvious verbal patterning (258–63). The consolations and remedies that Gaunt then goes on to offer, especially in lines 275–93, are ones that could have been found in many commonplace–books. This does not mean, however, that the speeches are lacking in emotion: Bolingbroke's replies, in particular, are resonant and charged with feeling, as in

> Oh who can hold a fire in his hand
> By thinking on the frosty Caucasus?
> (294–5)

But the emotions are held in control and decorously expressed. The scene ends with a patriotic flourish, as Bolingbroke takes his farewell of England (306–9).

As we have seen, the theme of language, and especially the discrepancy between language and thought, is prominent in the scene. Blood, in its various meanings, continues to play a large part in the imagery, and the scene also makes use of earth imagery (earth, ground, soil, fields, land). Blood and earth are linked by Richard when he gives his reason for exiling Bolingbroke and Mowbray: it is so that the earth of his kingdom shall not be soiled with the blood it has fostered (125–6). This also makes explicit the link between earth and England, repeated at the end of the scene in Bolingbroke's farewell to 'England's ground' and 'Sweet soil' (306). There are also images of feasting and of taste, especially sweet and sour (67–8, 92, 236, 296–7), which form one of the minor image-groups of the play.

Act I, Scene iv

Summary
King Richard and three of his friends, Aumerle, Bagot and Green, make malicious remarks about the banished Bolingbroke. Richard plans an expedition against rebels in Ireland, and, since he has run down his finances by extravagance, says that he intends to farm out his taxes and to extort money from rich men by means of blank charters. Bushy comes with the news that John of Gaunt is seriously ill; they take this as good news, and all go off to visit him.

Commentary
The scene opens in mid-speech, with Richard's 'We did observe' (1). It is quite common in Shakespeare for a scene to open in the middle of a conversation, but in *Richard II* it is rare. Here the usage marks a sharp contrast between Scene iv and the previous scenes. They had been formal and ceremonious, but this scene is marked by the absence of ceremony. We see people unbuttoned, see them as they really are underneath all the pomp and rhetoric: the mask is dropped, revealing the speakers' malice and their animosity towards Bolingbroke. The style accordingly is also pitched lower: in place of the heroic style there is witty and cynical speech. Richard and his friends are extremely amusing with their caustic observations, but this does not conceal their frivolity or their rancour.

The previous scene had ended with the parting of Gaunt and Bolingbroke. Here we begin with a parallel incident, describing Bolingbroke's departure from a different point of view. Aumerle's account of his parting from Bolingbroke (3–19) is about hypocrisy: the tear in his eye had been produced by the cold wind, not by grief; and he had been so unwilling to wish Bolingbroke well that he had pretended to be overcome by emotion and unable to speak. It is all very amusing, but also flippant and spiteful.

Richard utters a token rebuke to Aumerle for speaking in this manner about a member of the royal family, with his 'He is our cousin, cousin' (20). But the second 'cousin' implicitly concedes Aumerle's right to be thus critical, since he too is a member of the royal family. (He is son to the Duke of York, and so first cousin both to Richard and to Bolingbroke). But in any case Richard's mild rebuke is uttered only as a matter of form, for he himself goes on to make a scathing attack on Bolingbroke (21–36). This attack is political, condemning Bolingbroke for his 'courtship to the common people' (24), and revealing Richard's disquiet at his popularity. He even says (with unintended dramatic irony) that Bolingbroke behaves as if he were heir to the throne (35). The speech also reveals Richard's antipathy to 'the common people', for his scorn is directed at them as well as at Bolingbroke: he is clearly contemptuous of the poor craftsmen, the oyster-wench, and the draymen, and despises Bolingbroke for wooing them.

When they discuss the proposed Irish expedition (38–52) there is another disturbing revelation, this time about Richard's extravagance and financial mismanagement. For the first time, we learn about the political and economic reality beneath the brilliant surface of chivalry. Richard's account of the farming of his revenues, and his proposal to extort money by means of blank charters, give the audience their first inkling about his misgovernment. It is to be noted that Richard is not here led astray by his favourites: it is he who takes the initiative, not they. In this the play is in marked contrast to the anonymous play *Woodstock,* which was probably one of Shakespeare's sources: in *Woodstock* it is the favourites who make all the running, while the King is their dupe.

Even more shocking is Richard's callous and irreverent reaction when he hears of Gaunt's illness (59–64), hoping that God will inspire the physician to finish him off quickly, and that he will die before they reach his sick-bed. In the matter of seizing Gaunt's property, it is again Richard who takes the initiative (61–2), and the others simply echo him. Responsibility for what is done, and for its consequences, is thus laid firmly at Richard's door.

Throughout the play there are parallels and contrasts between the two leading figures, Richard and Bolingbroke. At this point, they are both about to go abroad, one into exile, the other to lead an army. When they return to England it will be Bolingbroke that leads an army. In the present scene, Richard is at a high point of his power, but the sympathies of the audience tilt away from him and towards Bolingbroke. For the first time, Richard's hypocrisy and political irresponsibility have been revealed to us, and Bolingbroke is seen as the innocent victim of his political animosity. The contrast between what people think and what they say has already been noted in Aumerle's false tears and feigned emotion (6–19), but in fact the whole scene brings out this contrast; after the rituals and the pretence of I.i and I.iii, we now learn what Richard and his friends really think and feel.

Act II, Scene i

Summary
John of Gaunt, gravely ill, is anxious to give the King his last advice
before dying. His brother York thinks that this will be useless: the
King's ears are stopped by flatterers. In an inspired prophetic vision,
Gaunt evokes England in all her beauty and splendour, and laments
that she is now mismanaged. Richard and Queen Isabel arrive with
many of the court. Gaunt utters a long reproach to Richard on his
misgovernment. Richard is furious. Gaunt is helped offstage by
Northumberland, who returns shortly afterwards to report his death.
Richard announces that he will forthwith seize Gaunt's estates to
finance his Irish expedition. York protests violently, but Richard
brushes aside his objections, and orders the seizure to be carried out.
He announces that he will set off for Ireland the following day, and
appoints York to be Lord Governor of England in his absence. The
King, the Queen, and the court go off, leaving only Northumberland,
Ross and Willoughby. These three lament Richard's misgovernment,
and Northumberland reveals secret news to them: Bolingbroke has
sailed from Brittany with eight ships and three thousand men, and
intends to land in northern England. Ross and Willoughby are fired
by this news, and all three resolve to ride immediately to meet
Bolingbroke.

Commentary
This scene is one of the emotional climaxes of the play, and is also a
major turning-point in the fortunes of the two central characters.
There are three passages of high emotional tension in the scene.
First, there is Gaunt's prophetic vision of England (31–68). The
temperature drops when the King and Queen enter, and Gaunt and
Richard play with words, but rises again with Gaunt's vigorous attack
on Richard's misgovernment (93–115), Richard's furious reply
(115–23), and Gaunt's final indictment of Richard as the murderer of
Gloucester (124–38). Emotions subside after Gaunt's exit, until
Richard announces his seizure of Gaunt's property, whereupon there
is an outburst from York, who makes a highly uncomplimentary
comparison between Richard and his father the Black Prince
(163–85), and protests violently against Richard's unconstitutional
behaviour in refusing to let Gaunt's son inherit (186–208). After
York's exit (214) the temperature drops again and remains low for
the rest of the scene, with just a little lift at the end when Ross and
Willoughby seize ardently on Northumberland's suggestion that they
should ride to meet Bolingbroke. Throughout the scene, and

especially in the three passages of high emotion, there is a rich deployment of the themes and image-clusters characteristic of the play, which often intertwine and interact with each other. Central to the scene is England — the needs of England, England as she has been and could be and as she is. The word *England* occurs no fewer than seven times in the scene, and the word *land* nine times (on all but two occurrences meaning specifically 'England').

The scene is a turning-point both for Richard and for Bolingbroke. Richard appears unassailable: Bolingbroke is banished, Gaunt dies, and Gaunt's estates can be used to compensate for Richard's previous financial mismanagement. But the seizure of Gaunt's estate turns out to be disastrous: it is this act more than any other that leads to Richard's fall. Like the heroes of many Shakespeare's tragedies, Richard takes an action which seems to ensure his safety, but which turns out to have the opposite effect. In the tragedies, moreover, it often happens that, when the central character has reached the peak of his power, he suffers a sudden sharp setback. This also happens in *Richard II*: at the end of the scene (277–300) we learn that Bolingbroke is already on the way back to England with a military force, and it is plain from the reactions of Northumberland, Ross and Willoughby that he will find a good deal of support when he arrives. It is to be noted that Bolingbroke and Richard are now moving in opposite directions (like the buckets in the well at IV.i.184–9): Richard is leaving England as Bolingbroke returns; and Bolingbroke is beginning to rise as Richard begins to decline.

The scene opens with a conversation between Gaunt and York which confirms the impression, gained by the audience in I.iv, that Richard is guilty of misgovernment and is led by flatterers. The speakers have no axe to grind, and are not polemical; they are elder statesmen who are anxious about the fate of their country, and the audience accepts their views at face-value. Their speeches pick up a number of the images that run through the play: harmony (6, 12), the sun (12), taste (13), poison (19), and above all language, and the relationship between language and reality (1–5, 7–9, 17, 26). Indeed, as the critic M. M. Mahood has pointed out, Gaunt's great speeches to Richard are framed between passages which identify speech with life: in the opening line of the scene, Gaunt's last breath is both his life and the counsel he wishes to utter to the King, and in line 8 he wishes to breathe ('utter') truth while he is breathing ('respiring') in pain; while later in the scene, when Northumberland announces Gaunt's death, he too identifies words with life (149–150).

Gaunt's great visionary speech on England (31–68) begins by evoking the glory of England (40–58) but ends with a bitter denunciation of the state that England has now been brought the King (59–68). In the earlier part, England is royal and maje and a source of military power (40–41), but is also the Garder Eden, the scene of nature's bounty, of innocence, of purity. This the only occurrence of the word *Eden* in the whole of Shakespeare's works, and it links the common garden imagery of the play to its religious themes. The speech emphasises the *earth* of England (41, 50) and the surrounding sea (46–9, 61–3), and introduces imagery of jewels (46) and of crusading (53–6), which will recur. The transition to the second part of the speech is marked by the bitter ambiguity of 'this dear dear land' (57), where *dear* can mean either 'held in affection, loved', or 'having a high price–tag'. The shame that England has come to is that she is now 'leased out' (59) as if she were a piece of private property like a house or a farm; the reference is to the King's expedient of selling his royal revenues to private individuals, who then extracted from the public the maximum taxes possible. *Bound in with* means both 'surrounded by'(61) and 'tied up in' (63), while *bonds* (64) means both 'legal documents which bind the signatory to pay sums of money' and 'shackles, chains, fetters'. The inky blots (64) are presumably the blank charters referred to at I.iv.48–50.

When the King and the Queen enter, there is a marked difference in the way they greet Gaunt; the Queen sounds both polite and concerned (71), while Richard sounds offhand, brusque, and barely polite (72). There follows a passage of word-play between Richard and Gaunt (73–92), ending with five lines of stichomythia. This passage, with its puns and antitheses and clever answers, seems slightly trivial after what has gone before, but it does carry on a major theme of the play, for it is about names and their significance and about flattery. Gaunt argues that his own name is a true reflection of what he is, and he implies that 'great King' (87) is not a true reflection of what Richard is.

At line 93 Gaunt begins his diatribe against Richard. The first two lines continue the quibbling mode, with the pun in *I see thee ill* (93) and the formal patterning on the words *see* and *ill* (94), but then Gaunt launches into an impassioned attack. He begins by developing the image of sickness: it is Richard that is ill, and England that is his death-bed; the quack–doctors that attend on him are his flatterers, who had been responsible for his illness in the first place (95–103). He then moves on to the theme of the family of Edward III, and links it with the idea of deposition, which here enters the play for the first time: if Edward III had foreseen the way in which his grandson Richard would destroy the members of his own family he would have

ed (disinherited) him before he had achieved possession of the
n. Gaunt then moves to another meaning of *possession* and
gests that Richard is insane (possessed by a devil) in such a way as
depose (disinherit) himself (104–8). The idea of deposition is put
into the audience's mind by the ultra-loyalist Gaunt, who would
never lift a finger against an anointed king, and this gives it all the
more force. Finally, Gaunt moves on to the specific behaviour which
has evoked his attack: Richard has leased England out, treated it as
though he were a landlord, not a king (110–14). The point that Gaunt
is making is that kingship is not a form of property-ownership: the
king has customary obligations and duties to his subjects, and his
country is not merely a source of income.

Richard is pale with fury: Gaunt's admonition drives the family
blood from his face. (There are suggestions in the play that Richard
has a very fair complexion, and pales and reddens easily.) It is
Gaunt's words which infuriate him – words which in this case are
obviously close to reality. His threat to execute Gaunt (121–3) is
quite shocking, made as it is to a reverend elderly gentleman who is
gravely ill, and who moreover is his uncle. The threat however
merely enables Gaunt to make a most telling riposte: Richard has in
fact shown no compunction about spilling the blood of Edward III's
family, having murdered his own uncle Gloucester (124–31). It is to
be noted that Richard makes no reply to this deadly accusation. From
the imagery of blood Gaunt moves on to that of natural growth, the
flower being cropped, another recurrent motif in the play.

When Gaunt goes off, Richard's comment is callous and churlish
(139–40), and York's attempt to pacify him (141–4) merely provokes
Richard into an expression of animosity towards both Gaunt and
Bolingbroke (145–6). When Gaunt's death is announced, Richard's
response is sententious and perfunctory (153–4), and he dismisses the
whole matter with his offhand 'So much for that' (155).

Whatever the historical truth, Richard's seizure of Gaunt's
possessions (160–2) is presented in the play as unconstitutional, and
indeed as an act of tyranny, as York's outburst shows (163–208).
York recalls the glories of the family of Edward III (171–83), as is
done so often in the play: he compares Richard with his father, the
Black Prince, and once again links blood relationship with the
shedding of blood (182–3). His argument against Richard's action
(190–208) is based on customary rights of inheritance, and he makes
the telling point that, in taking away Bolingbroke's hereditary rights,
Richard is undermining his own position as king. In effect, York
implies, Richard is setting a precedent for his own deposition, though
the word is not used. Nor does York mention rebellion, though this is

obviously the subject of the thoughts 'Which honour and allegiance cannot think' (208). The whole speech is most ominous for Richard, and makes his later exhortation to the Queen to 'Be merry' (223) sound somewhat hollow. But Richard is unmoved by York's arguments, and indeed takes his act of confiscation even further: originally, he had seized Gaunt's plate, coin, revenues and moveables (161), but to these he now adds Gaunt's 'lands' (210).

After the departure of the King and Queen and their followers, we have a passage where the Earl of Northumberland first emerges as a major force in the play. It was he who had helped Gaunt away (138) and who had announced his death (148–50), so he is obviously aligned with the Lancaster faction. Now he takes the lead in rebellion. At first he and Ross and Willoughby speak rather cautiously, and Ross says that he dare not utter freely what he feels (228–9). Northumberland, however, urges him to speak his mind, as does Willoughby. They then take it in turns to catalogue the King's misdeeds — his flatterers, his extortions, his extravagance, his weak foreign policy (238–61). When it is clear that they all have similar attitudes towards Richard, Northumberland, after some preliminary sounding (263–72), breaks the news to them· Bolingbroke is already on the way to England with an army (277–98). The list of gentlemen who are coming with him means little to the audience, but gives the feeling of a considerable body of support for Bolingbroke. The ultimate aims of the rebellion are left undefined: shaking off their slavish yoke (291) and wiping the dust from the gilt/guilt of the sceptre (294) could be done in various ways.

In this Northumberland–Ross–Willoughby passage, a new style enters the play. It is sounded immediately with Northumberland's 'Well, lords, the Duke of Lancaster is dead', and the reply 'And living too, for now his son is duke' (224–5). This is remote from the ceremonial style of the opening of the play; it is prosaic and matter of fact, and yet carries implications and suggestions below the surface meaning. The matter-of-factness of the style does not mean that it eschews figurative language: Northumberland expresses their danger in imagery of tempest, storm, wind (263–5). This imagery, however, is not expressed in formal patterns or ritual; nor does it resemble the witty word-play of I.iv, or of Richard and Gaunt playing with their names. Rather it seems to give a direct expression of the speaker's feelings, as in Northumberland's remarkable words

> Not so. Even through the hollow eyes of death
> I spy life peering   (270–1)

This is really quite an extravagant image, with life peering through the eye-sockets of a dead man's skull, but it creates with remarkable immediacy the speaker's sense of a possible new world and new life. It is to be noted that the line division occurs in mid-sentence, at a point where there is no natural break in speech, whereas in the more ceremonial and ritualistic passages in the play the line-endings tend to coincide with grammatical breaks.

The announcement of Bolingbroke's invasion involves a considerable foreshortening of time in the play. At the beginning of I.iv Aumerle has just taken his farewell of Bolingbroke; at the end of the same scene Richard learns of Gaunt's sickness and sets off to visit him. This visit takes place in II.i, presumably on the same day. But at the end of II.i we hear that Bolingbroke is already on the way back to England. This time-scheme is obviously quite impossible: Bolingbroke has hardly had time to set sail from England, let alone get to Brittany, hear of his father's death and organise an invasion. In historical fact, the abortive judicial combat of I.iii took place in September 1398; Gaunt died in February 1399; Richard sailed for Ireland in April 1399; and Bolingbroke landed in northern England in late June or early July 1399, not having sailed from Brittany until Richard had set out for Ireland. Shakespeare compresses these events for the sake of dramatic pace, and in the theatre the audience does not notice the impossibilities in the time-scheme.

Act II, Scene ii

Summary
Bushy tries to cheer up Queen Isabel in Richard's absence, but she has premonitions of disaster. Green brings the news that Bolingbroke has landed at Ravenspurgh and that many powerful men have gone to join him. York is engaged in raising forces to oppose Bolingbroke but has difficulties and is in a great fluster; moreover, his loyalties are divided, since Bolingbroke is his kinsman and has been wronged by the King. Bushy, Bagot and Green consider the situation hopeless; as favourites of the King they are in great danger, and Green and Bushy decide to take refuge in Bristol Castle while Bagot will go to Ireland to join Richard.

Commentary
Queen Isabel has so far spoken only one line in the play, and part of the function of this scene is to establish her and the role she is going to play. She sees her 'sweet Richard' (9) as a man, not as a political

figure, and by focusing attention on his personal qualities she will enhance the pathos of his fall. She also introduces the lyrical expression of grief, the indulgence in emotion, and the use of elaborate conceits which are later to be typical of Richard himself. The Queen's conversation with Bushy (1–40) is highly artificial, with its elaborate comparisons and its paradoxes: we are in a world of refined introspection and fantasy, in which the Queen plays with the idea of grief. The fantasy is shattered by the entry of Green (41) with his news of disaster, and the tone of the scene changes completely. The sharp decline in Richard's fortunes which began at the end of the previous scene now continues: Worcester too has gone to join Bolingbroke (58–60), and later in the scene we learn of the hostility of the commons to Richard (88–9, 128–31) and of the death of the Duchess of Gloucester (97), from whom York had hoped to obtain money.

York enters 'With signs of war about his aged neck' (74), and from this point until the end of III.iii the stage will be dominated by military figures. In the early part of the play there is brilliant spectacle, Richard's court in all its extravagance and flamboyance; but in the central part of the play we have a change to a more sombre costume, as men in military garb march and countermarch around the stage. York is flustered and at his wits' end, trying single-handed to raise forces against the rebels. Moreover, despite his loyalty to the crown, he has considerable sympathy for Bolingbroke, who has been wronged by the King; conscience and the claims of kinship both urge York to right that wrong (111–15).

York hints that Richard's flattering friends are likely to fail him in this crisis, and so it proves. At the end of the scene (122–48) Bushy, Bagot and Green are concerned only for their own safety. York had asked them to go and raise troops and to meet him at Berkeley (117–18), but they have no intention of doing anything of the sort: two of them decide to take refuge in Bristol Castle, and the third to go to Ireland to join the King (134–6, 140). They have already abandoned hope for Richard's cause (123–5, 144–6), and this reinforces for the audience the sense of the inevitability of Bolingbroke's triumph. They also express their fear of and contempt for the 'wavering commons' (128), the 'hateful commons' who will tear them to pieces (137–8).

Act II, Scene iii

Summary
Bolingbroke and Northumberland are marching with their army

through Gloucestershire, near Berkeley Castle, and are joined by Northumberland's son, Harry Percy, and by Ross and Willoughby. York comes out of Berkeley Castle and confronts them, accusing Bolingbroke of treason. Bolingbroke defends his actions; York agrees that he has been wronged, but argues that he should not right himself by force. York confesses that his army is too small to resist the power of Bolingbroke, and proclaims himself neutral in the conflict. Immediately afterwards, however, he invites Bolingbroke to spend the night in Berkeley Castle, an invitation which the latter accepts.

Commentary

It is now Bolingbroke, not Richard, who holds the centre of the stage. Richard is not seen between II.i and III.ii, and Bolingbroke emerges as a dominant figure. In the first part of II.iii we see his growing power and authority as he marches across England without meeting any opposition, being joined by powerful allies. In the second part of the scene we see his confrontation with York, and the powerful expression of their opposing political views. There is still no physical conflict, however, since York's forces are too weak to oppose Bolingbroke's. The significant conflict is that within York's mind: he is only too conscious of the force of Bolingbroke's case, and so he dithers, and eventually resigns himself to letting events take their course.

The scene opens with Northumberland indulging in fulsome flattery of Bolingbroke, itself a sign of Bolingbroke's power and status. Northumberland's style is now ceremonious again, with figurative language (centred on speech and sweetness) and verbal patterning (as at lines 15–16); this is the old politician in action, saying the right things to the man of the moment (though, not being a subtle man, Northumberland lays it on rather too thick). There follow three successive boosts to Bolingbroke's fortunes: the arrival of Harry Percy to join him (21–44); the latter's account of the pathetic weakness of York's forces in Berkeley Castle (53–6); and the arrival of Ross and Willoughby (57). To all of his supporters Bolingbroke replies courteously and with dignity, regretting his present inability to reward them for their help but promising to do so when his 'infant fortune comes to years' (66). In these speeches he strikes a note of deep sincerity, as in the lines

> I thank thee gentle Percy, and be sure.
> I count myself in nothing else so happy,
> As in a soul remembering my good friends.
> (45–7)

He may be saying the right things, but he does so with genuine personal feeling.

The second part of the scene begins when the Lord Berkeley comes with a message for Bolingbroke from York, and is sharply taken up for calling him 'Hereford' instead of 'Lancaster'. The whole basis of Bolingbroke's rebellion is his claim to his father's estates and title, which he says are being wrongfully withheld from him. This little interchange, with its insistence on 'name' (71), 'title' (72,75), and 'tongue' (72) carries on the theme of the relationship between words and reality, and specifically between names and their bearers. The message that Berkeley brings from York puts its emphasis on the peace of England, and the threatening of this peace by the rebellion (80).

When York enters, Bolingbroke kneels to him, but York rejects this gesture as 'deceivable and false' (84): we have seen the gap between words and reality, and now York calls our attention to a similar gap between reality and ceremonies of respect. York's long rebuke to Bolingbroke (86–104) emphasises the fact that the rebels are threatening the 'peaceful bosom' of England with war (91–4); invokes the concept of the 'anointed King' (95); and recalls the days of the Black Prince (98–104). This last passage, with its emphasis on York's present physical frailty contrasted with his former military prowess, carries on the theme of the generation gap which runs through the play. Bolingbroke's reply is polite and conciliatory (105–6), but when York persists in accusing him of treason he gives a long and eloquent defence of his actions (112–35). He begins with the change of title: he was banished as Duke of Hereford, but he comes back to claim his inheritance as Duke of Lancaster. He appeals to York's family feeling (114–21). He makes the telling point that his claim to be Duke of Lancaster rests on the same basis as Richard's claim to be King of England (122–3). And he demands his rights under the law.

Bolingbroke's followers give one-line echoes of support (136–8), and York himself obviously feels the force of Bolingbroke's arguments. Northumberland weighs in with the significant statement that Bolingbroke has sworn that his return to England has the sole purpose of obtaining his own rights. This continues to be the line taken by Northumberland and Bolingbroke (for example at III.iii.101–20, 196) until Richard actually abdicates in Act IV Scene i. When does Bolingbroke first make it his aim to become king? Early in the play, Mowbray had dropped a dark hint about Bolingbroke's treasonable intentions (I.iii.204–5); in the present scene, York plainly has forebodings, with his

> Well well, I see the issue of these arms.
>
> (151)

But the matter is left open, and we never really know what the long-term intentions of the rebels are, or at what point Bolingbroke decides to supplant Richard. The overall effect is to suggest that Bolingbroke is carried upward on a tide of fortune, seizing his opportunities when they come but very much the lucky beneficiary of events outside his control (such as the winds that delay Richard's return from Ireland).

York's dithering and indecision in the concluding part of the scene are positively comic. His loyalty to the legitimate king is so powerful that he would arrest the rebels if he could. Since he cannot, he declares himself neutral (157–8) – a fine decision for the Lord Governor of the kingdom to make! But even more comic is the fact that, in his very next breath, he invites Bolingbroke to spend the night in Berkeley Castle (159–60). It is a strange kind of neutrality which offers hospitality to the rebels! Bolingbroke announces his intention of going to Bristol Castle to deal with Richard's favourites there, the 'caterpillars of the commonwealth' (165). Here again, as in Gaunt's speeches in II.i, we have the image of England as a garden, but one which is ill-tended and must be taken in hand. Bolingbroke is here going somewhat beyond claiming his inheritance: he and his supporters are intent on putting the kingdom to rights. He wants York to accompany him to Bristol, but York is typically indecisive: perhaps he will, perhaps not (167–8); the rebels are neither his friends nor his foes (169); and his final note is one of hopeless resignation, with the knowledge that events are now out of his control:

> Things past redress, are now with me past care.
>
> (170)

Act II, Scene iv

Summary

A force of Welshmen have been waiting for ten days for Richard to return from Ireland, but have had no news, and intend to disperse. The Earl of Salisbury tries to persuade their Captain to wait one more day, but he refuses: there have been evil omens, he says, and it is believed that the King is dead. Salisbury foresees and laments the downfall of Richard.

Commentary

Richard's fortunes continue their rapid decline, as the Welsh waiting to support him gives up hope and disperses. It seems everything is against Richard, everything goes wrong; he is the victim of bad luck, delayed in Ireland by contrary winds (see II.ii.122- while Bolingbroke grows ever more powerful. The Elizabethans would have seen him as the victim of Fortune, whose wheel is carrying him down as it carries Bolingbroke upwards. We feel that there is something inevitable about Richard's fall, and this feeling is reinforced by the way in which his supporters give up hope at a very early stage – the Queen, Bushy, Bagot and Green (in II.ii), York (in II.iii), and now Salisbury (18–24). The feeling that Richard is on Fortune's wheel does however modify the audience's view of him: up to now there has been an emphasis on Richard's own moral and political responsibility for what happens; but now we see him to some extent as the victim of events.

The sense of impending disaster is heightened by the omens recounted by the Welsh Captain, fearful and unnatural happenings which portend social disorder and political change (8–15). Salisbury's final soliloquy uses elemental imagery: the King's glory is like a shooting star, falling from the region of fire to the earth; Richard is the sun, but the sun is setting and is weeping at the prospect of storms.

Act III, Scene i

Summary

Bolingbroke's forces have captured Bushy and Green; Bolingbroke gives a long account of their misdemeanours, and orders their execution. He leads his forces off to fight Richard's Welsh army.

Commentary

No word has yet been breathed suggesting explicitly that Bolingbroke may supplant Richard as king. Yet in this scene we see Bolingbroke behaving exactly as if he were already king: he gives orders, which he expects to be obeyed without question (1, 35, 37–9, 42–3), and these orders include the execution of two men. Moreover, when he gives an order it is in fact immediately carried out; this contrasts with Richard's ineffectual commands at I.i.162–86.

Bolingbroke's opening speech, arraigning Bushy and Green, is measured and controlled, and yet powerfully felt. He accuses them of misleading the King (8–10), following a long English political tradition of representing attacks on the Crown as attacks on the

...visers. The lines on Queen Isabel (11–15) are not entirely ...ey hint at homosexuality in Richard, but may merely mean ...s life of extravagant pleasure has led him to neglect her; but ...er interpretation is supported by anything else in the play. ...ally Bolingbroke comes to the wrongs which have been committed ...gainst himself, and here we have the expression of powerful personal feeling, in such splendid lines as

> And sighed my English breath in foreign clouds
> Eating the bitter bread of banishment.   (20–1)

These lines carry on the imagery of breath as speech and as life, and of taste, the bitterness of banishment being admirably brought home by the insertion of the concrete noun *bread*. The speech also continues the imagery of blood in its various senses (5, 9, 17, 26). The first of these examples, however, has a subtly undermining effect, for Bolingbroke washing the blood off his hands (5–6) inevitably reminds the audience of Pontius Pilate renouncing responsibility for the crucifixion of Christ (Matthew XXVII, 24–25). The implicit comparison with Pilate suggests that Bolingbroke is a conscientious but limited ruler, and hints moreover that Bushy and Green (and by association Richard too) are to be compared with Christ.

Northumberland, clearly the second-in-command, takes charge of the execution, and Bolingbroke turns to York to send a message to Queen Isabel (36–39): even in the life of a busy man of action, the courtesies due to others are not neglected. Finally, he sets in train the next bit of necessary action, a campaign against the Welsh. Presumably Glendower (43) is the Welsh Captain of the previous scene, the rebels not yet having heard that his army has dispersed.

The whole scene gives a picture of Bolingbroke as an efficient and reasonable ruler. Moreover, he continues to carry all before him apparently without effort: there is no suggestion that there was any violent struggle before Bushy and Green were captured at Bristol Castle; and when he marches off against the Welsh at the end of the scene the audience knows that this opposition too has already collapsed.

Act III, Scene ii

Summary
King Richard, returning from Ireland, lands on the coast of Wales. He asserts his invincibility as anointed king, but receives a series of shocks: he learns that his Welsh army has dispersed; that young and

old are defecting to Bolingbroke; that Bushy and Green have been exccuted; and finally that York and his forces have also joined Bolingbroke. At each piece of bad news, Aumerle and the Bishop of Carlisle encourage him to stand firm, but in the end he gives up hope, and orders his followers to be discharged; he himself will go to Flint Castle.

Commentary

One of the most striking things about the scene is Richard's volatility: he keeps swinging from exaggerated optimism to exaggerated despair, over-compensating at each switch; this is an aspect of his character which we have not seen before. These swings give the scene its shape: it consists of a series of peaks and troughs in Richard's feelings. The scene is also marked by a new style of speech in Richard: he speaks in exquisite lyrical poetry, in a melancholy and plaintive mode which can be described as elegiac. This manner is to be characteristic of him for the rest of the play. His poetry is highly-charged emotionally, with superb imaginative images, but tends to be self-centred, often with more than a touch of self-pity. It also calls our attention to Richard's obsession with language, which for him takes the place of action.

At the beginning of the scene we are back to pomp and ceremony, as it opens (according to the Folio text) with drums, a flourish of trumpets, and colours (banners). The stage-picture is still a military one, but the return of the King is marked by suitable display. Richard greets the 'Dear earth' of his kingdom with affectionate tears (4–6), but the audience is inevitably reminded of an earlier description of this 'dear dear land' (II.i.57) by Gaunt, and of his attack on Richard as 'landlord of England' (II.i.113). Richard's speech of greeting to his kingdom (4–26) is permeated with earth-imagery (6, 10, 12, 24), intertwined with images of tears (4, 9), sweetness (13), and poisonous things – spiders (14), venom (14), toads (15), nettles (18), an adder (20). The poisonous things are also products of the earth of Richard's kingdom, and he calls upon them to attack his enemies. This speech is eloquent and deeply felt, but it reveals Richard's propensity to deal in words rather than actions. Instead of getting to grips with the military and political situation, he utters invocations to the earth of his kingdom. Carlisle makes this point immediately (27–32): Richard is king by Divine Right, and God will keep him king however bad things may seem, but only if Richard uses the means which God offers him. In effect, Carlisle is urging Richard to *do* something, not just to talk, and in this he is seconded by Aumerle (33–5).

But Richard's response to this is to make another long speech

(36–62), asserting that the mere fact that he is a divinely ordained king is sufficient to defeat the rebels. He develops at length the parallel between the king and the sun ('the searching eye of heaven') (37–53): evils flourish at night, but when the sun rises (that is, when the true king re–appears in England) Bolingbroke will collapse in fear. He restates his belief in the invulnerability of a legitimate monarch:

> Not all the water in the rough rude sea
> Can wash the balm off from an anointed king.
> The breath of wordly men cannot depose
> The deputy elected by the Lord.   (54–7)

This affirmation of Divine Right is couched in two elemental images typical of the play: water (washing, the sea), and air (breath, speech, life). Richard ends by punning on the word *angel* ('coin' and 'heavenly spirit') and asserting that God's angels will fight for him and give him victory. Despite Carlisle's earlier admonition, Richard is still relying on God to do the work.

Salisbury's arrival with his bad news underlines the run of bad luck that Richard is having, the way in which Fortune's wheel is carrying him inexorably downwards: he has arrived 'One day too late' (67), and thereby lost a force of twelve thousand fighting men. Richard reacts by plunging from his previously vaunted belief in his invulnerability to complete despair: in a speech with a formal rhyme-scheme (76–81) he equates the blood of the soldiers he has lost with the blood that has fled from his cheeks, and tells his followers to abandon him. But it takes only one line of encouragement from Aumerle (82) to swing Richard's hopes up again: typically, it is the power of the king's *name* that he invokes: the simple fact of office is enough to defeat his enemies (83–9). Almost as an afterthought, he adds that his uncle York will surely have sufficient troops to serve his turn.

This brief peak of optimism is immediately dashed by the arrival of Scroop. Even before Scroop has given any firm news, but has merely indicated that the news is bad (91–2), Richard plunges again into despair. He simply gives up, resigning himself to the loss of his kingdom (95) and even to possible death (103), and falling back on the conventional comforts of philosophy (the loss of his kingdom will be the loss of care, he will remain equal with Bolingbroke in the eyes of God, death is in any case inevitable). It is to be noticed that it is Richard who constantly brings up the idea that he may be deposed by Bolingbroke: he had brought up the idea of deposition at line 56, and

now he plainly contemplates being supplanted by Boling
(95–9). By contrast, Bolingbroke and his followers have no
breathed a word about deposition.

Scroop's first news is that 'Both young and old' rebel agai.
Richard (104–20), and he begins with images of storms, river
overflowing their banks, the whole world dissolving into tears
(106–10). Richard had said earlier that not all the water in the rough
rude sea can wash the balm off from an anointed king (54–5), but in
this passage Bolingbroke is seen as threatening to do exactly that: he
is represented as water overflowing its limits (his proper place in the
social order) and flooding the whole country.

Richard enquires why his favourites have let Bolingbroke march
through England unopposed, and when Scroop says that they have
made peace with him (a euphemistic way of breaking the news of
their deaths gently) (128), he bursts into a hysterical denunciation of
them without questioning Scroop any further. In this outburst
(129–34) he links the theme of poisonous creatures (vipers, snakes)
with that of blood (his heart-blood). Moreover, by calling them
'Judases' (132) he implicitly identifies himself with Christ betrayed to
crucifixion. This identification has already been hinted at (III.i.5–6),
and is to be made quite explicit later in the play.

Scroop's explanation that Bushy, Green and Wiltshire have been
executed by Bolingbroke identifies the earth with the grave (140), an
aspect of the earth imagery which is prominent in the rest of the play.
Richard makes no response to this news, neither expressing grief nor
retracting his violent attack on his favourites: he seems to be sunk in
apathy. It is left to Aumerle to try to get back to business by asking
Scroop where York and his forces are (143), but Richard does not
even wait for an answer, and instead plunges into the long despairing
speech beginning 'No matter where, of comfort no man speak'
(144–77).

In this speech we see Richard's new elegiac style at its most
compelling, and it is surely one of the really great passages in the
play. An analysis of the speech is given in Section 5 below. Here let
us simply note that the last poignant passage of seven lines (171–7) is
a psychological turning point in the play. For the first time, Richard
has realised the difference between Man and Office, and speaks of
the things he has in common with other people rather than the things
that set him apart from them. The recognition comes too late to save
Richard from disaster, but this is the moment in the play when the
audience's sympathies swing decisively towards him. For the rest of
the play, whatever his weaknesses, he is seen in a sympathetic
light.

sle and Aumerle once again try to pull Richard together and
ade him to take action, and Aumerle reminds him that York has
rmy (178–87). The volatile Richard once again swings upwards
o an exaggerated optimism, with 'An easy task it is to win our own'
91). But despite Richard's adjuration (193), Scroop's sour looks do
not conceal sweet speech, and he delivers the final blow to Richard's
hopes with his news of York's defection to Bolingbroke and the
almost universal support for the latter (194–203). Richard reproaches
Aumerle for having led him out of the 'sweet way' to despair which
he had been in, and finally gives up hope (203–18). He orders his
soldiers to be discharged: he is now barren ground, and they will do
well to *ear* ('plough') the land where there is some hope of growth;
this land, plainly, is Bolingbroke, who by implication is now
identified with England. Richard also rejects all 'flatteries of [the]
tongue' (216), another recognition which has come too late, and
repeats the order to disperse his soldiers:

> Discharge my followers: let them hence away
> From Richard's night, to Bolingbroke's fair day.
> (217–18)

This contrasts strikingly with the earlier part of the scene: in lines
36–53, Richard had seen himself as the sun rising in majesty,
terrifying the thief Bolingbroke who had revelled in the night. But
now it is Bolingbroke who is the day (the rising sun), and Richard
who is sinking into night.

Act III, Scene iii

Summary
Bolingbroke, York and Northumberland arrive with their army at
Flint Castle, and learn that King Richard is there. Bolingbroke sends
Northumberland with a message to Richard, who appears on the
battlements. Northumberland tells the King that Bolingbroke swears
that his sole object is to obtain his rightful inheritance, and that when
this is granted he will disband his forces. Richard comes down into
the courtyard and meets Bolingbroke, and virtually offers to resign
the crown to him. They set off for London.

Commentary
The scene is spectacular, with Richard on the battlements of Flint
Castle like the 'blushing discontented sun' (63), while on the earth
below is the military power of his opponents. The rebel army perhaps

marches around the stage while Northumberland approaches the castle and speaks to the King, for Bolingbroke orders it to march upon the grassy carpet of the plain so that the people in the castle can see its 'fair appointments' (49–53): clearly he thinks that it is a splendid sight. The climax of the scene comes when the sun-king descends 'like glistering Phaeton' (178) and meets Bolingbroke in the courtyard below; it is the first time the two men have met since I.iii.248. The scene deals in hypocrisies and pretences: both sides conceal their true feelings and intentions under diplomatic language, until Richard breaks through the pretence and reveals the ambitions of the rebels, which have so far remained unexpressed. In his face-to-face encounter with Bolingbroke, Richard recognises the reality of power, and submits to the necessities of power-politics (190–209).

The scene opens with a brisk and business-like exchange between Bolingbroke and Northumberland about the military situation, which contrasts strongly with the wordiness and impracticality of Richard in the previous scene. There follows York's protest at Northumberland's improper reference to the King as 'Richard' instead of 'King Richard' (7–19) This brings out the ambiguity of York's position: he has joined the rebels, but still regards Richard as a 'sacred king' (9), and reminds Bolingbroke that the Heavens are over their heads and that he should not take more than is legally due to him (16–17). York obviously believes that Bolingbroke's ambitions now extend beyond the restitution of his inheritance, and this passage makes the audience think so too. We have already seen Bolingbroke behaving as if he were king, issuing commands and having men executed (III.i); now Northumberland's 'Richard' reveals what the leaders of the rebellion really think and intend: for them, Richard is finished as king; and there can be no doubt as to who they intend shall replace him. The passage is a brief one, but the impact on the audience's perception of the rebels is considerable; one result is that for the rest of the scene all of Bolingbroke's assertions about his loyalty to Richard and the innocence of his intentions are seen by the audience as hypocrisy.

The message which Bolingbroke entrusts to Northumberland (31–61) is full of such assertions, and of ritual ceremonies of respect (kissing the King's hand on both his knees, showing his stooping duty), but they are accompanied by conditions ('Provided that . . .'); and the conditions are accompanied by a clear threat of force, a vision of the earth of England drenched in its native blood. The speech is diplomatically phrased, but the iron hand is obvious beneath the velvet glove, and the threat is made tangible by the marching of the rebel army in its splendour under the walls of the castle. The speech ends by invoking the elemental forces of fire and water in a thunderstorm (54–60), Richard being the fire and Bolingbroke the water; Bolingbroke says that he will be the *yielding* water, but it is to be noted that the water is seen as raining on the earth (obviously bringing fertility and prosperity), while the lightning merely expends itself in 'rage'.

Richard and his few remaining followers appear on the battlements of the castle (that is, on the balcony or gallery above the back-centre of the stage) (61). Despite the smallness of their numbers, the entry is made with pomp and ceremony, with trumpets answering trumpets; and the sense of occasion is reinforced by the comments of Bolingbroke and of York, with their images of Richard as the sun and as the eagle (62–71). Richard's long speech of rebuke to Northumberland (72–100) is controlled and majestic, and yet, after the events of the previous scene, the audience surely has the feeling that he is now play-acting, playing the part of the king as he knows it should be played, even though the reality of power has slipped from him. He demands from Northumberland the proper ceremonies of respect due to a king (72–6), asserts that God alone can depose him (77–81), and ends with a powerful prophetic vision of England torn for generations by civil war and bedewed with English blood (85–100). This prophecy refers to the events of the *Henry IV* plays, the *Henry VI* plays and *Richard III*: it sees these events as the result of Bolingbroke's desire for the crown (95), and this usurped crown will not live in peace until ten thousand Englishmen have had 'bloody crowns'. Although he has just asserted that only God can depose him (77–81), this prophecy in fact assumes that Bolingbroke is going to depose him. This is typical of Richard in his decline: there is a constant conflict in his mind between the real world and the world as he wishes it to be or thinks that it ought to be.

Northumberland conveys Bolingbroke's message (101–20), with promises certified by oaths (105, 119), but by this stage the audience is probably disinclined to believe him, and sees the promises as hypocrisy. Richard joins in the game of hypocrisy (121–6), especially in saying that his noble cousin Bolingbroke 'is right welcome hither', but immediately reveals to Aumerle that he dislikes the game, suggesting that instead they should fight and die (127–30). Aumerle, however, argues that they must 'fight with gentle words' until such time as they have swords to fight for them. The theme of hypocrisy, the gap between words and meanings, is here explicit.

When Northumberland returns from Bolingbroke, Richard launches into one of his long speeches of self-pity and self-abasement

(143–75), in which he seems to enjoy playing with the situation, weaving little webs of fantasy around it. He is not Aumerle's advice to 'fight with gentle words'; on the contrar, giving up hope, accepting submission and deposition (143–4), mercy of 'King Bolingbroke' (173) (which, however sarcastic meant, is still handing everything to his rival on a plate). The spee is marked by highly formal rhetorical devices, and especially by the figures of speech in which intricate verbal patterns are produced by the use of repetition (see Section 4.6 below). This patterning is very obvious in lines 147–53, where each line repeats a common structure ('My A for a B'), but it permeates the whole speech. This elaborate use of rhetoric makes the speech seem somewhat literary: whereas in the previous scene Richard had really been overwhelmed by despair, he now seems to be playing with the idea, and decorating it. This is borne out by the fancifulness of some of his conceits, such as that of the two kinsmen digging their graves with their tears (164–9), or creating such bad weather with their sighs and tears that they ruin the harvest (161–3).

Northumberland returns with Bolingbroke's invitation to Richard (in effect a command) to meet him in the 'base-court', and there follows one of the great symbolical moments of the play, the descent of Richard from the battlements to meet Bolingbroke on the ground below:

> Down, down I come, like glistering Phaeton,
> Wanting the manage of unruly jades.
> In the base-court? base court, where kings grow base
> To come at traitors' calls, and do them grace.
>
> (178–81)

Richard identifies himself with Phaeton, whose unskilful attempt to drive the chariot of the sun brought him to disaster. The fall of Phaeton is mimicked by the language, with its wonderful juxtaposition of the poetic and the commonplace: after the splendid resonant rhetoric of line 178 we come down to the colloquialism of the 'unruly jades' in line 179. The fallen Richard then vents his feelings in bitter puns on the words *base* and *do them grace*.

When Richard and Bolingbroke meet, the latter continues the charade of faithful duty by kneeling (189), but Richard rejects this courtesy as unsuitable for Bolingbroke's status and ambition (190–5). The latter repeats his assertion that his sole object is to obtain his legal inheritance (196), but Richard's response is 'Your own is yours, and I am yours and all' (197). The point is often made that Richard elf out of the crown: it is he who raises the question of ...n and refers to King Bolingbroke long before the rebels ...ny such overt suggestion, and he frequently seems bent on ...struction, on giving away his royalty before he is even asked. ...the other hand, his attitude at this moment in the play can be ...erpreted as realism, and a determination to tear down the curtain of hypocrisy with which the rebels are concealing their true aims. He certainly recognises the facts of power:

> They well deserve to have
> That know the strong'st and surest way to get.
> ....
> For we must do what force will have us do.
>
> (200–1, 207)

The only question is: does Bolingbroke in fact already intend to usurp the throne? If the audience believes that he does, they will not see Richard's attitude at this point as defeatism, but as an acceptance of the inevitable. This interpretation is supported by Richard's correct reading of Bolingbroke's next move, to take him to London (208). He obviously has a clear idea of what to expect when they get there.

Act III, Scene iv

Summary

Queen Isabel and two of her ladies are in the Duke of York's garden, weighed down with melancholy. They eavesdrop on a Gardener and his two assistants, who contrast the good order in their garden with the disorder in the commonwealth. The Gardener tells his assistants that Bolingbroke has captured the King, who is likely to be deposed. The Queen emerges from hiding and confronts the Gardener, who confirms this news. The Queen curses the Gardener for his ill-tidings, while he pities her plight.

Commentary

The scene is obviously not realistic: the Gardeners do not talk like real gardeners (compare them, for example, with the grave-diggers in *Hamlet* or Bottom and his crew in *A Midsummer Night's Dream*), and it is to be noted that they speak in verse, not prose. The scene is a dramatic expansion of one of the central images of the play, that of England as a garden. The garden and the Gardener are therefore symbols or emblems, standing for a country and its ruler, and the scene can be described as symbolic or emblematic. The metaphor of England as a garden draws on a number of the image-clusters of the play, notably earth, plants and flowers, weeds, generation and growth, and (via the Garden of Eden) religion. These images interact all through the scene, and even the image of blood is brought in, by the identification of the sap of trees with the blood of aspiring noblemen (59). The scene has a simple and symmetrical structure, falling into four parts: (1) the Queen and her two servants converse; (2) the Gardener and his two servants converse; (3) the Queen's party confronts the Gardener's party; (4) the Queen and her followers depart, so that the scene ends, as it began, with only one group holding the stage.

In the first section (1–23), the Queen rejects the various suggestions made by her two ladies for pastimes to relieve her melancholy, in every case introducing some clever reason for her rejection. This is an elegant and courtly playing with the idea of grief, parallel to Richard's in the previous scene. The Queen's speech is mannered and patterned, as can be seen especially clearly in lines 11–18. The section ends with repeated references to tears and weeping (20–3).

In the second section (29–71), the Gardener at once suggests the parallel between the garden and a country, with his references to an 'executioner', 'our commonwealth', and 'our government'. The first servant makes the comparison with England quite explicit (40–7). His phrase 'our sea-walled garden' (43) reminds us of Gaunt's description of England earlier in the play, the 'other Eden' which is defended by 'the silver sea, /Which serves it in the office of a wall' (II.i.42–7); and this inevitably reminds us too of Gaunt's denunciations of Richard's misgovernment. The suggestion that the garden of England is 'Swarming with caterpillars' (47) takes our minds back to the 'caterpillars of the commonwealth' denounced by Bolingbroke (II.3.165) and now destroyed by him. Bolingbroke is seen by the Gardener as the saviour of the garden of England, plucking up the weeds (50–2), whereas Richard had neglected it and let it go to ruin (55–66).

When the Queen comes forward and confronts the Gardener, she addresses him as 'old Adam's likeness' (73), identifying the garden with Eden. The parallel is continued with Eve, the serpent, and the Fall of Man (75–6); she sees the imminent deposition of Richard (which is news to her) as a second Fall. She therefore identifies Richard with Adam, and so (indirectly) with Christ, since theologians called Christ the Second Adam. In his reply, the Gardener develops the image of a pair of scales, in which Richard is outweighed by Bolingbroke and the English peers (84–9)

The Queen has hardly been polite to the Gardener, addressing him as 'thou little better thing than earth' (78) and cursing his plants because he has brought her bad news (100–1); admittedly she is under emotional stress, but even so we can see her contempt for the lower orders of society as typical of Richard's court. The Gardener, however, repays cursings with blessings, and in the brief final section of the scene (102–7) he plans to plant a bank of rue 'In remembrance of a weeping Queen' (107).

Part of the function of the scene is to evoke pity for the Queen's plight, to bring out the pathos of her situation, and this will be carried further in her scene of parting from Richard (V.i). But even more important is the function of the scene in bringing us firmly back to the politics of Richard's deposition, and reminding us of his misrule, his neglect of the garden of England. In this later part of the play much attention is given to Richard as a man, and to his emotional problems in the face of disaster. This scene counterbalances that emphasis with a reminder of what Richard has been and what he has done.

Act IV, Scene i

Summary

In Parliament, Bolingbroke investigates the circumstances of Gloucester's murder; accusations and counter-accusations are made, and challenges issued. York brings the news that Richard has resigned the crown to Bolingbroke, and hails the latter as King Henry IV. Carlisle makes a long speech of protest; he is charged with treason. Richard is brought into the Parliament, and formally unkings himself. Northumberland orders him to read out a list of his crimes, but he evades this demand, and reproaches the bystanders as traitors. He calls for a looking-glass, in which he seeks his own identity. He is taken away to the Tower. Bolingbroke sets a day for his coronation, and Parliament disperses. Carlisle, Aumerle and the Abbot of Westminster plot a coup against Bolingbroke.

Commentary

The scene falls into four main sections: Bolingbroke's attempt to get to the bottom of Gloucester's murder (1–106); Carlisle's protest at Bolingbroke's assumption of the throne (107–53); the long and complex passage in which Richard renounces his kingship and abdicates in favour of Bolingbroke (162–321); and the brief

concluding section in which Carlisle launches a conspiracy a
new king (322–35).

The scene opens with a ceremonial entry of Bolingbroke a
peers to Parliament. It is an irony that in this 'new world' (7
business-like government we should still find the pomp a
ceremony of the older world. Things have changed, however. Th
uttering of challenges and throwing-down of gages (19–85) offer a
clear parallel to the opening scene of the play, when Bolingbroke and
Mowbray similarly exchanged defiances and threw down gages. Now,
however, it is Bolingbroke who presides over the proceedings, not
Richard; and Bolingbroke conducts affairs in a decisive fashion, and
expresses himself in a direct and forthright style (as in the opening
speech of the scene). Bolingbroke, however, is not seated on the
throne, even though he has taken charge of matters and behaves as if
he were already king: the throne is certainly there on the stage, but
Bolingbroke does not offer to mount it until line 113. Moreover, the
accusations that are thrown back and forth lack both the ceremonial
quality and the heroic style of the challenges in I.i; by comparison
they seem petty in tone.

Bolingbroke makes a firm decision: the challenges shall remain in
suspense until Mowbray's exile has been repealed and he has come
home to testify (86–90). He is frustrated, however, by the news that
Mowbray has died in Italy after long and honourable service in the
Crusades (91–100). We are therefore left in ignorance about the
murder of Gloucester. Mowbray, formerly accused so vehemently by
Bolingbroke, is now presented sympathetically as a soldier of Christ,
and Bolingbroke wishes rest to his soul (103-4). Suspicion does
indeed fall on Aumerle, who has been accused by four people and
defended by one, but there is no certainty that he is guilty. So even
the efficient Bolingbroke has failed. Moreover, the parallel with the
first scene suggests that he has inherited some of Richard's problems,
notably a bunch of squabbling peers, which he does not wish (see,
for example, lines 158–61).

As can be expected, the whole of this opening passage is shot
through with ideas of speech and truth – lies, slander, falsehood,
tongue, lips, breath and so on -- and plainly carries on the theme of
the gap between speech and reality.

The news of Richard's agreement to abdicate is, significantly,
brought by York (107–112). York is an elder statesman, the last
surviving son of Edward III, and is respected for his loyalty and
devotion to duty. His participation in the public replacement of one
king by another gives the action a kind of respectability: it is not a
hole-and-corner affair, but is being conducted by proper

nal means. His announcement begins by addressing
oke as 'Great Duke of Lancaster' and ends by hailing him as
ienry IV, thus marking the moment of change. After his long
d of vacillation, York is now devotedly loyal to Bolingbroke, as
ormerly was to Richard, and continues so for the rest of the play.
is case underlines the strains to which men of good intentions are
subjected when there is a challenge to the legitimacy of established
authority, and his fierce loyalty to Bolingbroke (as seen later in V.ii
and V.iii) suggests a certain relativity in both legitimacy and
loyalty.

No such relativity is admitted, however, by Carlisle, who in his
long and eloquent speech of objection (114–49) puts forward a
traditional Divine Right view: the king is 'the figure of God's
majesty' (125), his 'captain, steward, deputy elect' (126), and his
subjects have no power to judge or sentence him (121–2). He goes on
to a powerful vision of England racked by civil war, its ground
manured by the 'blood of English' (137), culminating in an
identification of the country with the 'field of Golgotha and dead
men's skulls' (144), a reference that once again suggests that Richard
is Christ crucified. Carlisle's protest, made at the very moment that
Bolingbroke is about the ascend the throne, reminds the audience
that there is still an opposition viewpoint, and that Bolingbroke's
accession is destined to produce discord, and make England more
like a charnel-house than like the Garden of Eden.

Richard turns his abdication (162–318) into a star performance in
which he upstages everybody else present. He is indeed in distress
and confusion, and swings between different attitutudes, sometimes
abasing himself, sometimes breaking into bitter denunciations. And
his attention is still focused on himself and his own sufferings. But he
is a natural actor, and obviously loves to perform in public, and
especially to turn everything into ceremonies and symbolic acts. He
also loves words, and makes long speeches while Bolingbroke replies
in single lines. From the start he takes the initiative, first in attacking
the bystanders as Judases and comparing himself with Christ (170),
and then in stage-managing the little episode in which he and
Bolingbroke each hold one side of the crown (181–9). In this last
speech he introduces the telling image of the two buckets in the well,
which seems to sum up the whole course and structure of the play. He
continues with formally patterned speech (191–202), with neat
rhymes and antitheses; Bolingbroke replies in single lines, which
Richard caps with rhyming lines (191, 195); the exchange ends with
Richard's pregnant wordplay on *ay* and *I* (201–2). The speech in
which he divests himself of kingship (203–22) uses highly patterned

rhetorical figures, as in the solemn sequence of lines beginning 'With mine own . . . ' (207–10), and in the insistence on the Richard–Bolingbroke antithesis (214–19). In this speech Richard is consciously reversing the coronation ceremony which made him king, inventing a kind of de-coronation ceremony.

After the eloquence and splendour of this speech, Northumberland's interposition (222–7, 243) sounds brusque and tactless. His demand that Richard shall read out a list of his 'grievous crimes' provokes Richard into a bitter denunciation of his opponents (232–42, 244–52), in which he again identifies himself with Christ (239–42); but, having denounced his enemies as traitors, he recognises that he himself is also a traitor, since he too has consented to the undecking of 'the pompous body of a king' (247–52). Northumberland persists in pressing Richard, but his 'My Lord–' (253) sets the latter off on another tack: he is no man's lord; indeed, he has no name or title. Richard, who has acted the part of king for so long, has lost his role and feels that he has lost his identity. Indeed, his final piece of acting has had precisely the effect of depriving him of his role and of his name, so that he feels a non-person. This feeling is beautifully captured in the image of the snowman (260–2): it is now Bolingbroke who is the sun-king, and Richard is merely the effigy of a king made of snow, melting away as if in tears.

Richard's sense of his loss of identity leads on to the celebrated episode of the mirror (276–302). There is something typically narcissistic about Richard's examination of his face in the looking-glass, but clearly, having lost his social function, he is trying to fathom who or what he is. He finds that his sorrows are inadequately written in his face: he ought not to be able to recognise himself. The mirror, therefore, is a flatterer, as his followers were in his days of prosperity, and he evokes the glory of those days:

> Was this face the face
> That every day under his household roof
> Did keep ten thousand men? Was this the face
> That like the sun did make beholders wink?
> (281–4)

This echoes a famous line from Christopher Marlowe's *Dr Faustus* ('Was this the face that launched a thousand ships?'), spoken by Faustus when Mephistopheles gives him a vision of Helen of Troy. So Richard's words not only evoke the glory of his past, but also suggest its destructiveness, just as the idea of feasting ten thousand men reminds the audience both of the magnificence of Richard's court and of the wanton extravagance which contributed to his downfall. But that glory has proved as brittle as the mirror, which Richard now dashes to pieces on the floor: he has found no new image in the looking glass to replace the one which has gone.

Richard now directly addresses Bolingbroke, the 'silent King' (290) who has looked on all this time, and who, in a stage performance, acts as an enigmatic and powerful counterbalance to Richard by his mere silent presence. Bolingbroke has been tolerant of Richard's act, even indulgent. When Northumberland, in his usual blunt manner, keeps insisting that Richard shall read his list of crimes, despite the fact that Richard is in a state of near-hysteria, Bolingbroke quietly and tactfully asks him to desist (269–71). Now he makes a sensible and penetrating comment on Richard's 'moral of this sport' (290–3), and this drives Richard to a deeper apprehension of his sorrow:

> My grief lies all within,
> And these external manners of laments
> Are merely shadows to the unseen grief
> That swells with silence in the tortured soul.
>
> (295–8)

These lines are quite different from the elaborate rhetorical devices with which Richard has hitherto spoken of his sorrow, and have a real inwardness of feeling. Bolingbroke continues to be polite and considerate to Richard (304–16) until the latter finally departs for the Tower with a bitter jibe at the bystanders (playing on the word *convey*) as his exit-line (317–18). Bolingbroke then promptly puts the whole performance behind him, with a brisk two-line instruction about his coronation which concludes the business of the meeting (319–21).

In the brief concluding section (322–335), Aumerle, Carlisle and the Abbot of Westminster plan a counter-plot against Bolingbroke. The moment Bolingbroke achieves the crown, he suffers his first setback, in the form of a conspiracy against him. This is parallel to what had happened to Richard: when he was at the height of his power, having banished Bolingbroke and seized Gaunt's property, he was immediately threatened by a conspiracy, initiated by three men (II.i.224–300). The play contains many such parallels between the two central characters. The plot against Bolingbroke is destined to fail, but it bodes ill for the future of his reign.

Act V, Scene i

Summary
Queen Isabel meets Richard as he is being conducted to the
and they say goodbye. Northumberland comes with an order
Bolingbroke that Richard is to be taken to Pomfret, not to
Tower, and that Queen Isabel is to be sent to France. Richar
prophesies future division between Bolingbroke and
Northumberland. Richard and Isabel take a final farewell and part.

Commentary
The scene consists of a prelude (a solo passage by Queen
Isabel)(1–10), followed by an A–B–A structure. The 'A' passages
(11–50, 71–102) are laments and partings between Richard and
Isabel, while 'B' (51–70) is the interlude with Northumberland.

In the 'A' sections, the emphasis is on the personal, on the pathos
of Richard's situation and the parting of husband and wife. The
laments and the leavetakings are however highly ceremonious, and
the style is decorative and fanciful rather than heartfelt. A good
example of this fancifulness is Richard's speech imagining Isabel
telling his sad story by the fireside (40–50), ending with the conceit
that the burning wood-logs in the fire will 'weep' with compassion
and put the fire out, some of them mourning in ashes and some
coal-black for Richard's deposition. Tears and weeping run all
through the 'A' passages, so that the overall effect is stylised but
lachrymose.

By contrast, the 'B' passage is political. Richard's prophecy of
contention between Bolingbroke and Northumberland is extremely
acute, and persuasively argued. It foresees exactly what is to happen
in the *Henry IV* plays. The prophecy is given even greater force by
the words spoken by Northumberland on his entrance four lines
earlier ('My lord, the mind of Bolingbroke is changed'). Not 'King
Henry', but 'Bolingbroke'. Richard has obviously read correctly his
attitude to the new king. Northumberland's answer to Richard's
prophecy is a shrugging off of moral responsibility under the pretence
of accepting it ('My guilt be on my head, and there an end') (69).

After this scene, Richard does not appear again until Act V, Scene
v. There is indeed nothing more for Richard to do or suffer apart
from his final attempt to come to terms with reality in V.v, followed
by his murder. The intervening space is filled out with the lower-key
and less distinguished scenes dealing with the Aumerle conspiracy
and the incitement of Exton to the murder of Richard.

y

uke of York describes to his Duchess the triumphant entry into
.don of Bolingbroke, followed by Richard, who had been jeered
. (This entry had taken place before Act IV, Scene i.) Their son
Aumerle comes in, and York notices and seizes a sealed document
that Aumerle has in his doublet. It reveals a treasonous plot against
Bolingbroke, and York immediately calls for his boots, so that he can
ride to the King and reveal it. The Duchess tries to dissuade him, but
in vain. She tells Aumerle to take his father's horse and get to the
King before him, to ask for pardon. She will follow to second him.

Commentary

The first part of the scene (1–40), York's account of the entry of
Bolingbroke and Richard into London, continues the process of
building up sympathy for Richard; the lower his fortunes fall, the
more the audience is invited to feel pity for him and to admire some
of his qualities. This passage is particularly effective in doing this
because Richard himself does not speak. When Richard holds forth
on his griefs he gains the audience's sympathy by his sheer eloquence
and by his intensity of feeling, but he also tends to lose sympathy
because of his emotional volatility, his tendency to pity himself, and
his disregard of his own share in the responsibility for his fall. York's
account by contrast shows Richard behaving in a humble, patient,
and self-controlled manner, and being treated vilely by the
spectators. Typically, however, the picture of Richard is balanced by
one of Bolingbroke, the latter being given fifteen lines (7–21) and the
former fourteen (23–36). Moreover, the picture of Bolingbroke is by
no means an unsympathetic one. York concludes the section by
reminding the Duchess that, whatever their feelings for Richard, they
are now 'sworn subjects' to Bolingbroke, whose right to the throne
they accord and concur with ('allow') for ever ('for aye') (39–40).

In the remainder of the scene, in which York discovers Aumerle's
implication in a plot to murder Bolingbroke, we move into sheer
comedy. York is a trifle comic earlier in the play, and now the
comedy blossoms, with his triple calling for his boots (77, 84, 87), the
Duchess's attempt to stop his servant from giving them to him (85–6),
and her hustling of Aumerle out to steal his father's horse and get to
Bolingbroke before him (112–14). Earlier in the play, Gaunt had
proclaimed his loyalty in solemn religious terms (I.ii.4–8, 37–41), but
that ceremonious world has now gone, and York proclaims his loyalty

by shouting for his boots. The effect of the episode is to cast doubt on the absoluteness of loyalty (and therefore of a ruler's legitimacy), and it is fitting that York, who has changed from one loyalty to another, should create this effect. The scene also contributes to the theme of the generation-gap: the older generation (Gaunt, York) are loyal to established authority, while their sons (Bolingbroke, Aumerle) rebel against it.

Act V, Scene iii

Summary
Bolingbroke, now King Henry, enquires for news of his dissolute son, and is given some by Harry Percy. Aumerle rushes in and asks for a private audience, which the King gives him. Aumerle kneels and asks for pardon, which the King grants. Aumerle locks the door to prevent interruption while he tells his story, but York arrives and bangs on the door, and the King lets him in. York shows the King the document he had taken from Aumerle. The Duchess arrives, and she and York compete in pleas to the King, she asking for Aumerle to be pardoned, he for Aumerle to be executed. The King confirms the pardon he had promised to Aumerle, but arranges for the arrest and execution of the remaining conspirators.

Commentary
The opening part of the scene (1–22), in which we learn of the dissolute life of the King's son, has a double function: it prepares the way for the Hotspur–Hal opposition in *Henry IV Part I*, and also interposes necessary material between Aumerle's exit at the end of the previous scene and his entry in this scene. (On the Elizabethan stage it was hardly possible for a scene to end with a character walking off, and the next scene to begin with the same character walking on.)

The exchanges (23–72) between the King and Aumerle, with York later joining in, are perfectly serious. The fact, however, that the King has already promised to pardon Aumerle (32–4) takes some of the tension out of the situation: the outcome is fairly certain and so the audience is not in any great suspense about it, despite the pleadings and counter-pleadings. The King underlines the theme of the generation-gap ('O loyal father of a treacherous son')(59), and is obviously quite unconscious of the parallel with himself (Gaunt the loyal father and Bolingbroke the treacherous son). When the Duchess in turn arrives to bang and shout at the door (73–7) the comic elements in the situation take charge, and the scene becomes very nearly farcical. The King comments on the change ('Our scene is altered from a serious thing')(78), and now that he is quite obviously in no danger he allows himself a sardonic dig at Aumerle ('My dangerous cousin, let your mother in')(80); the nicely-chosen word *dangerous* combines a reminder to Aumerle of his moral guilt with a slightly patronising dismissal of him as ineffectual. The pleadings to the King by York and the Duchess (82–129) are almost exclusively concerned with words, and the relationship between words and thoughts: just as Gaunt had spoken in favour of Bolingbroke's banishment without really wishing it (I.iii.236–46), so York (according to the Duchess) is now being hypocritical in urging the condemnation of Aumerle (99–109). There is also a good deal of kneeling. The play as a whole makes great use of ceremonies of respect, but here the kneeling and counter-kneeling are comic, and so undermine such ceremonies. The Duchess kneels when she first enters, and steadfastly refuses all requests to her to stand; then Aumerle kneels to second her plea (96), whereupon York promptly kneels to oppose i (97). They all continue to kneel, despite the King's 'stand up' (110, 128), until Aumerle's pardon has been confirmed not once but twice (130, 135), whereupon they presumably all rise. After this comic interlude the King turns back to serious matters, and, in his usual decisive and business-like manner, gives orders for the arrest of the remaining conspirators (136–42).

Act V, Scene iv

Summary
Sir Piers of Exton, in conversation with his servants, reveals that the King has obliquely incited him to murder Richard in Pomfret Castle. They set off to ride to Pomfret.

Commentary
This brief scene is a necessary preparation for the murder of Richard: it would be puzzling for the audience if Exton burst in and killed him without previous explanation. The scene also indicates the King's involvement in the murder, however indirectly he may have phrased himself. In the following scene (V.v), while Richard is trying to puzzle out his problems, the audience is aware that Exton and his servants are already on their way to Pomfret, which creates suspense.

Act V, Scene v

Summary
Richard, in prison in Pomfret Castle, makes an elaborate comparison
between his prison and the world; he imagines himself playing many
social roles; he hears music outside, and recognises his own
responsibility for the breaking of harmony in the state. He is visited
by a poor stable-groom, who expresses his grief that Bolingbroke has
ridden on Richard's favourite horse. The groom is sent away by the
Keeper, who brings Richard a meal; the Keeper, however, refuses to
taste it first, and says that this is on the orders of Exton. Richard
attacks the Keeper; Exton and his servants rush in; Richard kills
some of them but is himself killed by Exton. Exton expresses remorse
for the murder, and sets off to take the body to the King.

Commentary
Richard's long opening soliloquy (1–66) is in part an attempt to get to
grips with his situation, to establish an identity for himself, but in part
an evasion of it. He begins with an elaborate and ingenious
comparison between his prison and the world (1–30); here he is
playing with words and with ideas, which he is making into a
substitute for reality. This looks like an attempt to escape from his
problems, but it leads on to a passage about role-playing (31–41) in
which he imagines himself in different roles (king, beggar); he has
always been an actor, but now he clearly acknowledges the fact. He is
not contented, however, in any role that he imagines for himself, but
decides that this is the common human fate, and that the only easing
of any man's discontent is death ('being nothing') (41).

At this point the outside world breaks in on his thoughts, as music
plays outside. Richard immediately develops the comparison
between music and 'men's lives', and especially between musical
harmony and the harmony of the commonwealth (41–50). And here,
perhaps for the first time, he explicitly recognises his own share of
political responsibility for the misfortunes which have overwhelmed
him:

> And here have I the daintiness of ear
> To check time broke in a disordered string:
> But for the concord of my state and time,
> Had not an ear to hear my true time broke,
> I wasted time, and now doth time waste me:
> (45–9)

That final line is one of the most telling in the play. The neat rhetorical pattern is a common enough one, but is given especial force by the change of meaning in the verb *waste*. It is also given force by the whole context: Richard is finally admitting that as a private individual (listening to music) he can detect a false note, but as a king he had no ear for the discords in the government and welfare of his realm. Unfortunately for Richard, the recognition of this truth, like some of his other recognitions, has come too late; indeed, for the audience, Salisbury's 'One day too late' (III.ii.67) seems to echo through the rest of the play.

After this moment of truth, Richard continues to meditate on time (50–60), but he has now turned inward again to his own sufferings ('clamorous groans which strike upon my heart . . . sighs, and tears and groans')(56–7), and the comparison between his own grief and Bolingbroke's 'proud joy' leads to the sudden outburst at 'This music mads me' (61). Almost at once, however, he calms down; moreover, he turns outward from himself in gratitude to the provider of the music ('Yet blessing on his heart that gives it me')(64); this is the first time we have seen Richard reach out to bless somebody else.

The episode with the stable-groom (67–97) continues the building up of sympathy for Richard as a man. Richard's court, we have seen, was rather disdainful of ordinary people, but here is a humble groom who has taken considerable trouble ('much ado')(74) to visit him out of love. And Richard responds, with his 'gentle friend' (81) and his solicitude for the groom's safety (96). It is gently amusing that the groom's greatest distress has been caused by the riding of 'roan Barbary' by Bolingbroke (76–80), but this gives us yet another parallel between the latter and Richard, and gives Richard the opportunity to consider the ingratitude of animals and of men (84–94).

The final episode of the scene, the murder (98–118), begins with the Keeper refusing to taste Richard's meal; this was a normal precaution against poisoning, and Exton's command suggests that he has poisoned the food. Richard certainly seems to think so, and this is the moment when his patience finally snaps. He has cultivated the Christian virtue of patience for a long time: Queen Isabel had reproached him for it (V.i.26–34); York had praised him for it (V.ii.23–36); but now 'Patience is stale' (103) and Richard assaults the Keeper (with the carving-knife, according to Shakespeare's main source). The poisoning having failed, Exton and his followers rush in to kill Richard with weapons. Richard obviously makes ferocious resistance: he kills one man with his own weapon (106), and the later reference to 'the rest' of the dead bodies (118) shows that he has

killed at least two men and probably more. This is the
violent physical action in the whole play, and, typically, ı.
late: if Richard had shown such determination and figh.
when he landed from Ireland, the audience feels, things mig
turned out differently. In his dying lines (108–12), Richard us
elemental imagery so common in the play – the fire of Hell for Ex
the king's blood staining the earth; moreover, by referring to himse
as 'the King', he asserts once again his inalienable right to the crown.
Exton's admiring comment ('As full of valour as of royal blood')
reminds us that the blood he has spilt is that of the family of Edward
III, and that Richard's behaviour has for once been worthy of his
ancestry.

Act V, Scene vi

Summary
King Henry receives news that various rebels against him have been
defeated and executed. Exton arrives with the body of Richard, but
Henry condemns his deed and refuses to reward him. Henry leads the
mourners who follow Richard's coffin.

Commentary
The whole scene is pitched in a very low key, and is little more than a
tidying-up now that the major events of the play are over. The first
part of the scene (1–29) is a necessary buffer between Exton's exit at
the end of the previous scene and his entry at line 30. It informs the
audience of the failure of the conspiracy against Henry and the
execution of the rebels; Henry thus ends the play in a strong position,
but at the same time the rebellions against him are ominous, and
remind us of the prophecies of future trouble made by Carlisle, who
is indeed now present on the stage. Henry's merciful treatment of
him (24–9) is a statesmanlike recognition of Carlisle's courage and
constancy to his principles.
   Henry's rejection of Exton (34–44) is a masterpiece of political
equivocation: he profits from the murder, but tries to escape moral
responsibility for it ('They love not poison that do poison need'). In
the final Biblical reference of the play, he identifies Exton with Cain,
the first murderer, who killed his brother Abel; but it does not escape
the audience that Henry has in effect identified himself with Cain, for
it was he who inspired the murder, and the victim was his own cousin.
There is also a parallel between Henry (responsible for the death of
his cousin) and Richard (responsible for the death of his uncle
Gloucester), and the audience may even recall that Henry himself,

.e latter murder, had identified Gloucester with Abel
nis final speech of regret(45–52), Henry combines two of
.on images of the play, blood and vegetation (plants,
on, growth, gardens); but the combination is grotesque, with
,gestion of blood being sprinkled on a plant to make it grow
, a procedure which seems highly unnatural. Henry's desire to
piate his blood-guilt by going on a pilgrimage to the Holy Land
,49–50) carries on a minor theme of the play, and one which is to
recur in the *Henry IV* plays. The play had begun with a ceremonial
entry by Richard and his court; it ends with Richard making a
ceremonial exit in his coffin, with his rival and successor leading the
funeral cortege.

3 THEMES AND ISSUES

3.1 MEDIEVAL AND MODERN

E.M.W. Tillyard has argued that *Richard II* depicts the brilliant court-life of the late Middle Ages, and the supplanting of that way of life by a more modern and practical one. He emphasises the extreme formality of the play both in shape and in style, and its highly ceremonial quality: the poetic language is exquisitely patterned; actions tend to be symbolic rather than real, everything being turned into ceremonies; the direct or naturalistic presentation of strong emotion is avoided, and use made instead of convention and conceit (that is, fanciful notions or comparisons); and the numerous cosmic references in the play are extremely elaborate and formal. The ritual element, moreover, is central to people's behaviour: the precise manner in which a thing is done is more important than what is done. Means matter more than ends.

It was in the Middle Ages, Tillyard argues, that the rules of the game of life were elaborated in this way, and *Richard II* is Shakespeare's picture of that world; for information about it he was indebted to Lord Berners's translation of Jean Froissart. But the world of medieval refinement is threatened, and in the end superseded, by the more familiar world of the present. The conspirators, when acting as such, do not use the ceremonial style of Richard's court, but a plainer, more vigorous and more passionate mode of speech. Bolingbroke and Northumberland belong to a new order, where people act decisively to get things done, and often feel passionately about them.

Against this view it has been argued that Bolingbroke himself uses a high rhetorical style, and takes part in the elaborate formalities of the judicial combat, in Act I of the play, and this is obviously so. At this stage he is still part of the old order, but when he and the other

3.3 MAN AND OFFICE

The play constantly contrasts the man and his office, the individual human being and his social role. The critic E. H. Kantorowicz has suggested that Shakespeare's handling of this theme was influenced by the legal doctrine of 'the king's two bodies', which distinguished between the king's natural, mortal body and his legal existence as ruler. Kantorowicz sees the play as a tragedy of dual personality, in which the fiction of the king's double body gradually breaks apart; and he examines various 'geminations' or 'duplications' in Richard: King and Fool, King and God, God and Fool.

Whatever may be thought of Kantorowicz's particular analyses, he is clearly right about the doubleness of the king's nature. Richard is an actor, playing out an allotted social role. The idea that he is an actor is made explicit in York's description of his entry into London (V.ii.23–6), in which Richard's welcome is compared to that given to a second-rate actor in the theatre immediately after a star performer (Bolingbroke) has gone off. Richard himself makes the comparison in his final long soliloquy ('Thus play I in one person many people') (V.v.31); here he acknowledges his own role-playing, whereas at the beginning of the play his acting had been unconscious: he had completely identified himself with his role of king, and saw no separation between his person and his function.

The social roles that people play are intimately bound up with their sense of identity, and when Richard loses his social function as king he feels that he has lost his identity, become a non–person. This feeling is notably expressed in the mirror episode (IV.i.275–99) and in Richard's striking image of himself as a snowman melting away in the sun of Bolingbroke (IV.i.259–62). His final soliloquy (V.v.1–66) can be seen as an attempt to find an identity for himself in a world which has become incoherent. In the early part of the play, Richard's identity is established by his unambiguous position in a stable and hierarchical society; but now, not only has he lost that position, but the society itself has changed: the sense of a divinely-ordained order has crumbled before the military power of Bolingbroke, and the elaborate games and ceremonies of Richard's court have given way to the commonsense practicalities of the new order. Richard is left in a chaos, in which he makes his individual effort to re-establish some kind of order in the universe; this he does by trying to re-order his own being, his inner universe, since the world outside appears to be beyond repair.

Not all is loss for Richard, however: in his deprivation he comes to greater self-knowledge. There are two main stages in this, which provide turning-points in his development: first, his recognition of his own humanity, and secondly his belated recognition of his own share of responsibility for his disasters. The first turning-point is in III.ii, when, on his return from Ireland, he cries out to his friends to abandon the ceremonies of respect with which they treat him,

> For you have but mistook me all this while:
> I live with bread like you, feel want,
> Taste grief, need friends: subjected thus,
> How can you say to me, I am a King?
> (III.ii.174–7)

Here for the first time Richard recognises that, beneath the pomp of kingship, he is a man, with basic human needs like other men. The second turning-point comes in Richard's final soliloquy, when he acknowledges that he has had no ear for the 'concord of his state and time', and ends with the confession

> I wasted time, and now doth time waste me.
> (V.v.49)

Up to this point, Richard has blamed anybody but himself for the evils which have befallen him; now, at last, he recognises the truth, and accepts at any rate some of the responsibility. The growth in Richard's recognition of his own humanity is accompanied by an increase in the audience's sympathy for him: the somewhat repellent king of the early part of the play becomes the fascinating and often pathetic human being of the final acts. The quality of Shakespeare's dramatic art is seen in the skilful way in which he controls our feelings about Richard and our attitudes towards him.

Closely linked with the theme of Man and Office is the extensive use in the play of names and titles. In the early part of the play, sonorous titles like 'Harry of Hereford, Lancaster, and Derby' (which occurs three times in I.iii) establish clearly the place of the title-holder in the social hierarchy. They also, by their frequent and accepted use, establish the fact of the social hierarchy itself, and its everyday acceptance by the speakers. But as the order of Richard's England begins to break down, names and titles sometimes change, reflecting changes in people's status. Richard himself sets off the process by trying to prevent Bolingbroke from inheriting his rightful title of Duke of Lancaster. Bolingbroke, understandably, is extremely touchy about this title, as when Berkeley addresses him as 'My Lord of Hereford' (II.iii.69–73). In the end, Richard's attempt rebounds on himself; Northumberland, even before the formal deposition, refers to him unceremoniously as 'Richard' (III.iii.6); and after the deposition Richard complains that he has no name, no title, and no longer knows what name to call himself (IV.i.254–9). This loss of his name is associated with his sense of a loss of identity, for he immediately continues with the snowman image and the mirror episode. When Bolingbroke changes his title from Duke of Lancaster to King Henry, his attempt to establish a new order with himself as head includes at least one change of title among his subjects, that of Aumerle to Rutland (V.ii.41–3).

3.4 LANGUAGE AND REALITY

A theme that runs all through the play is the relationship between words and things, and between speech and action. In particular, we are constantly invited to contemplate the gap between what people say and what they really think, the disjunction between language and reality. The play is full of lies, broken oaths, and hypocrisy. In the very first scene, when Mowbray and Bolingbroke hurl their accusations at one another, it is clear to the audience that at least one of them must be lying; Richard calls our attention to this, when he says 'Yet one but flatters us' (I.i.25). There is a similar situation later in the play, when various noblemen, in Parliament, accuse one another of lying and slander (IV.i.1–85). Nor is it always possible for the audience to divine the truth: we are never given any absolute certainty, for example, about Mowbray's role in the murder of Gloucester. Some examples of the clash between language and truth are less culpable: when John of Gaunt says that his vote for his son's banishment had been contrary to his real desires (I.iii.236–46), he is simply calling attention to an inner conflict, and to his different reactions as a father and as a statesman (Man and Office once again); there is a parallel situation later, when York urges that his son Aumerle shall be condemned, and his Duchess argues that he does not really mean it (V.iii.99–109). On the other hand, when Bolingbroke breaks the oath made on his return from exile (that he has come merely to claim his rights as Duke of Lancaster)(II.iii.147–50, III.iii.105–20, 196), the audience must see this as a grave offence and judge Bolingbroke accordingly.

Richard more than anyone else is concerned with language and reality. It is often said that he is a poet, and he is certainly in love with words. Indeed, he seems to have a belief, in the earlier part of the play, in the almost magical efficacy of words. When he says that 'Lions make leopards tame' (I.i.174), he obviously believes it: his enunciation of the fact practically makes it so. Later, he asserts the divinity of kingship, and his own invulnerability (for example III.ii.36–62). His statement of this fact, which he sees as a truth about the nature of the universe, is by itself sufficient: he does not feel the necessity for decisive action which is urged on him by his friends (as at III.ii.27–35).

This belief in the potency of language would have seemed less surprising to the original audience than it does to us. There was a strong traditional view which held that there is a natural relationship between words and what they denote; that this indeed is something built into the logic of the universe. When an author set out to treat some subject, he normally had a set of categories ('topics') to help him to find material; one of these categories was 'the name'; so, when Sir Philip Sydney set out to write a defence of poetry, one of the first things he discussed was the word *poetry* and its significance; and this was not just padding: language was not purely arbitrary, but was related to the essences of things.

In the course of the play, however, Richard loses his belief in the efficacy of words. This change is forced on him by the failure of his words to control reality. It is Bolingbroke who is able to control and to change things, and for Bolingbroke words are not magical or inherently effective, but are instruments to be used. For him it is actions which are effective, and he acts while Richard talks. For, even though his words fail to control events, Richard continues to be in love with them right to the end. Indeed, his love of language helps to bring about his downfall: at Flint Castle he practically hands the crown to Bolingbroke (III.iii.190–209), at a time when Bolingbroke has made no mention of wishing to seize it, and is indeed still maintaining the charade of loyal devotion to Richard. This suicidal behaviour of Richard's is emphasised by Shakespeare's departures from his sources (see Section 4.1).

4 DRAMATIC TECHNIQUES

4.1 USE OF SOURCES

The main source for *Richard II* was Raphael Holinshed's *Chronicles of England, Scotland, and Ireland* (1577), of which Shakespeare used the enlarged edition of 1587. He probably drew as well on Edward Hall's *Union of the Two Noble and Illustre Families of Lancaster and York* (1548), which begins at the same historical point as the play and imposes a strong moral and political pattern on history. Minor sources probably include Samuel Daniel's poem *The First Four Books of the Civil Wars* (1595) (which influences Shakespeare's treatment of Queen Isabel), the anonymous play *Woodstock* (c. 1592-5)(which handles the murder of the Duke of Gloucester), and Lord Berners's translation of Froissart's *Chronicles* (1523-5). These sources provided raw material, which Shakespeare shaped into a play. By selecting, compressing, changing the order of events, inventing new episodes, and sometimes departing completely from the historical facts as recorded, he produced a structured work of art, giving his own imaginative interpretation of the events in question.

The reign of Richard II is full of exciting and dramatic happenings, but Shakespeare chose to deal only with its last two years, from April 1398 to March 1400; this puts the deposition of Richard at the centre of interest, and makes it the major theme of the play. Within this period, many events are omitted because they do not contribute to the main story-line of the play (for example, Richard's doings in Ireland). Others are omitted for reasons of dramatic economy: there is no scene, for example, showing Bolingbroke's coronation as Henry IV. The transfer of power had already taken place in the deposition-scene (IV.i), and a coronation would have contributed nothing further. Moreover, the pomp and display of a coronation would have associated Henry with old-fashioned ceremony such as had ruled at Richard's court, which would have been inappropriate for the 'new world' (IV.i.78) of the Lancastrian monarchy. Much more in character is Bolingbroke's quite unceremonious proposal that he should 'ascend the regal throne' the moment he hears that Richard has agreed to abdicate (IV.i.113).

Some omissions, however, have greater implications, and affect our interpretation of events: a notable example is the deception of Richard by Northumberland at Conway Castle. According to Holinshed, Richard and his friends, after their return from Ireland, went to Conway Castle; Northumberland came to them there and offered terms from Bolingbroke: a Parliament should be assembled, and certain reforms carried out, whereupon Bolingbroke would submit obediently as a subject to Richard. Richard accepted the terms, and agreed to ride to meet Bolingbroke, but Northumberland had set an ambush, and Richard was captured and taken to Flint Castle as a prisoner. Shakespeare's omission of this episode (which is also omitted from Hall's account) has the effect of making Richard's conduct at Flint Castle (III.iii) seem much more indecisive and self-destructive. It also makes the conduct of the Bolingbroke faction appear less treacherous.

The process of selection and compression also involves the foreshortening of time and the amalgamation of different episodes. The foreshortening can be seen between the end of I.iii and the end of II.i: it is quite clear that there just has not been time for Bolingbroke to get to Brittany, let alone send a message to say that he is about to come back to England with an army. In the theatre, however, the audience does not notice the discrepancy, and it has the effect of speeding up the pace of the action. The amalgamation of episodes can be seen in IV.i: this combines events which, according to Holinshed, took place on no fewer than four different days. Moreover, their order is altered: the plot by the Abbot of Westminster is moved to the end of the scene. This has the effect of making Richard's abdication the centre-piece of the scene, while the Abbot's plot becomes a sudden setback for Bolingbroke immediately after his triumph, and also prepares us for the events of Act V.

Actual changes to historical events are often made to obtain greater dramatic impact: thus Richard himself is made to pronounce the sentences of exile on Mowbray and Bolingbroke (I.iii.123–53), whereas historically they were read out to them by a herald; and in the deposition-scene (IV.i) Richard is brought in person into Parliament to confront Bolingbroke and to make a formal abdication, whereas in historical fact he signed the articles of abdication in prison. The use of Queen Isabel to build up pathos is made possible by a change in her age (in which Shakespeare may be following Daniel): historically, the Queen was only about ten years old at the beginning of the play, and about twelve at the time of the deposition; Richard in fact never met her again after the parting at Windsor when he set off for Ireland. Some changes are probably motivated by a desire to prepare the way for the *Henry IV* plays: Northumberland is made to play a larger part in the return of Bolingbroke than he did historically, and his son Harry Percy is much reduced in age, in preparation for his confrontation with Prince Hal.

Considerable changes, moreover, are made in people's characters. Richard himself is Shakespeare's own creation. Gloucester, who is referred to in the play as if he were a plain, honest, well-meaning man, is described by Holinshed as being fierce, hasty, wilful, and warlike. John of Gaunt, depicted in the play as a wise elder statesman, was in fact ambitious and scheming: far from being unquestionably loyal, he and York raised forces after the murder of Gloucester and contemplated action against the King. But Shakespeare needed a character to represent the 'divine right' and loyalist point of view, and to admonish Richard on the error of his ways, and Gaunt filled the bill. In the chronicles, as in the play, Bolingbroke is a slightly enigmatic figure, and it is difficult to pin down the moment when he decided to aim at the crown; but it is noteworthy that, according to Holinshed, many noblemen and others wrote to him while he was in exile asking him to come back and promising to help him to expel Richard and to make himself king. Shakespeare makes no mention of this, thus helping to keep Bolingbroke's motives unclear.

Many episodes in the play are entirely of Shakespeare's invention. These include Gaunt's scene with the Duchess of Gloucester (I.ii), Gaunt's deathbed scene (II.i), the Garden scene (III.iv), the episodes where Richard and Bolingbroke hold the crown (IV.i.181–3) and where Richard calls for a mirror (IV.i.264–91), the parting between Richard and Isabel (V.i), and the passages involving the Duchess of York (V.ii, V.iii). Here Shakespeare's imagination puts flesh on the bare bones of history.

4.2 STRUCTURE

The structure of the play resembles that of many of the great tragedies which Shakespeare was to write from the turn of the century onwards. In these, there is normally a central character (the protagonist) whose fortunes rise until some point near the middle of the play, and then decline again until he ends in disaster and death.

Immediately after reaching the highest point in his fortunes, the protagonist often suffers a sudden sharp setback. During the period of decline, there are often episodes which evoke pathos (the death of Portia in *Julius Caesar,* Ophelia's madness and death in *Hamlet,* the murder of Lady Macduff and her children in *Macbeth).* In this part of the play, too, the protagonist often indulges in introspection and self-analysis; commonly, however, he is kept off the stage for a considerable period in Act IV or thereabouts (partly perhaps to give the actor a necessary rest). Within the rise-fall pattern there are smaller rhythmic fluctuations of fortune, which help to create suspense. The protagonist usually has some admirable qualities, which win the audience's respect, but suffers from some fatal flaw which (combined with ill fortune) leads to disaster.

It will be seen that *Richard II* conforms to this pattern in many ways. The protagonist, Richard, reaches a peak in his fortunes in II.i (rather early in the play compared with the great tragedies), with Bolingbroke banished, Gaunt dead, and the Lancaster estates seized to finance his Irish war. At the end of the same scene, however, there is a sudden sharp setback with the conspiracy of Northumberland, Ross, and Willoughby, and the news that Bolingbroke is on his way back to England. Thereafter Richard's fortunes decline steadily, though with some fluctuations, notably in III.ii. During the decline, pathos is produced by the episodes involving Queen Isabel, especially the parting from Richard (V.i), and he indulges in a positive orgy of introspection (though perhaps not self–analysis). Richard is kept off-stage from the end of V.i to the beginning of V.v (though it is to be observed that he is also kept off-stage for a considerably longer period earlier in the play, from II.i.223 to III.ii.1).

Richard II, then, has structural resemblances to Shakespeare's later tragedies. But it also differs from them in a major respect: it has two central characters, not one, and the two are opposed to each other. In the tragedies, there is often a character or group of characters opposed to the protagonist (Antony and Octavius to Brutus, Claudius to Hamlet, Iago to Othello), but such characters are subsidiary: the protagonist is the centre of attention. But in *Richard II* there are two central characters, Richard and Bolingbroke, and their fortunes are mirror images of one another: Richard's rise and fall are exactly matched by Bolingbroke's decline (exile, seizure of his estates) and rise. The play thus has a double plot-structure, and this is emphasised by the use of parallel incidents: for example, both Richard and Bolingbroke leave England early in the play, one with an army and one going into exile, but when they return it is Bolingbroke who has the army: they both preside over a session in which noblemen denounce and challenge one another about the murder of Gloucester (I.i. and IV.i), and both are frustrated in their attempts to settle the matter; and both, immediately after reaching their highest point of power in the play, are subject to a conspiracy against them (II.i.224–300, IV.i.322–35).

The double plot of *Richard II* explains why it is possible for Richard to be kept off-stage for so long in Acts II and III: in this part of the play it is Bolingbroke who takes the centre of the stage, counterbalancing Richard's earlier domination of it. It also helps to explain why there is practically no comedy in the play. In the later plays of the *Henriad* there is a main plot (dealing with high-life characters, politics, and war) and a sub-plot (dealing with comic low-life characters and their escapades); the sub-plot tends to parody the main plot or make implicit comments on it. But in *Richard II,* with its double main plot, there is no place for a sub-plot, and the only comedy is provided by York and his dilemmas.

The use of parallel incidents and situations in the play is not confined to the contrast between Richard and Bolingbroke. For example, there are parallel father–son pairs, Gaunt–Bolingbroke and York–Aumerle: the older generation preaches divine right and loyalty, while the younger generation rebels. In addition, the play makes use of symbolic or emblematic scenes or incidents. The garden-scene (III.iv) is quite unrealistic, and provides a kind of expanded metaphor: England is a garden which has been ill-tended; the gardeners themselves are a model of good government. Other obviously symbolic incidents are Richard's holding of the crown between himself and Bolingbroke, and the mirror episode, both in the deposition-scene (IV.i): these give vivid visual and dramatic expression to themes of the play.

4.3 IMAGERY

When Shakespeare critics speak of 'images' (or collectively of 'imagery'), they can mean various things. An image can be a metaphor or other figure of speech. Or it can be a phrase which creates a vivid picture. Most often, however, critics mean *iterative* (repetitive) imagery. In Shakespeare's plays there are always recurrent words or groups of words which affect the atmosphere of the play, point to the themes it is handling, and shape the audience's responses. An image in this sense often forms part of a metaphor or other figure of speech, and sometimes offers a vivid picture. But it does not necessarily do either. For example, one of the dominant images in *Richard II* is blood, but many of the references are quite

literal (the blood shed when Gloucester was murde
be shed in civil war). A minor image-group in the pla.
references to taste, and especially to sweet and sour;
occur as metaphors, but in the nature of things they obvic
provide any visual image.

Richard II is marked by a considerable advance in Shakesp
use of imagery. It is characterised by what Richard D. Altick
called 'symphonic imagery': certain groups of words, some of the.
words of multiple meaning, others of sensuous significance, recur
throughout the play; each word-group symbolises one or other of the
fundamental ideas of the story, which it extends and enriches: and the
various word-groups are constantly mingling and coalescing,
especially at critical moments in the play, producing new figures and
emphasising the complex relationships between the ideas
themselves.

Many of the image-groups have been discussed and illustrated in
the account of individual scenes in Section 2.3 above; you can find
further examples yourself while working on the play. Here it is not
necessary to do more than give a summary of the word-groups you
will be looking for.

Andrew Gurr has pointed out that many of the common images in
the play can be classified as examples of the four elements (earth, air,
fire, water), and some as examples of the four humours (melancholy,
blood, choler, phlegm). One of the common fire-images is the sun,
which was both a common symbol for kingship and also a particular
emblem used by Richard himself. Richard's sun is threatened
by the clouds and storms of Bolingbroke (as at III.ii.106–9 and
III.iii.54–60), which include water (rain, overflowing rivers) and air
(winds). Water also occurs frequently in the play as the sea and as
tears, while air appears as speech and as sighs. Earth is particularly
associated with England (the government and welfare of which are a
major concern of the play), and also with graves and tombs. The four
elements were arranged in a hierarchy, with fire at the top and earth
at the bottom; Richard begins at the top, as sun-king, but in the
course of the play he descends through the elements (like glistering
Phaeton at III.iii.178), so that we find him sitting on the ground
telling sad stories of the death of kings (III.ii.155) or contemplating
graves and dust and earth (III.ii.145–50, III.iii.153–9, 167–9), until
finally he falls dying on his own land (V.v.110).

Of the four humours, the major one in the play is blood (the word
blood occurs no fewer than 41 times, and *bloody* six times). It is often
used literally, for example, in the many references to the murder of
Gloucester (as at I.i.103–4), but it is also used to refer to kinship

_), and especially to the descendants of Edward III,
.s were like 'seven vials of his sacred blood' (I.ii.12).
.ant interplay between the literal and kinship meanings
murder of Gloucester is discussed, since Richard
.ter's nephew) is assumed to be responsible for the murder.
.so provides a link with the Biblical imagery of the play, via the
y of Cain and Abel (as at I.i.104). Blood imagery is linked to
.rth imagery by the frequent threats or prophecies of the shedding
of blood on English soil, in judicial combat or in civil war. Blood is
also used to denote qualities of temperament, especially when people
have an excess of it (as at I.i.153) or a deficiency (as at I.ii.10).

Blood in the sense of kinship is part of a group of images dealing
with generation and conception, seen, for example, in Queen Isabel's
speeches at II.ii.34–40, 61–5; and this group is linked to the idea of
inheritance, including figurative uses (what the future will inherit
from the present, for example). One of the metaphors for
family-relationship is the *branch* of a tree (as at I.ii.18), and this links
the blood and kinship images with another group extremely
prominent in the play: there is constant reference to natural growth –
fruit, flowers, trees. In particular, there is much garden-imagery,
which extends far beyond the garden-scene, including references to
plucking and cropping and withering, and to things inimical to
gardens such as weeds and caterpillars. Gardens are also part of the
earth–imagery, and the garden is a metaphor for England; Richard's
favourites are called the caterpillars of the commonwealth
(II.iii.165), and the same image occurs in the garden-scene
(III.iv.47). Since England is a 'sea-walled garden' (III.iv.43) it
consists of the element of earth protected by the element of water.
Before Richard's misgovernment it was the Garden of Eden (II.i.42)
– the only occurrence of the word *Eden* in the whole of Shakespeare.
This links the garden-imagery, via Adam (III.iv.73), with the Biblical
references in the play. These include the Cain and Abel story (used of
the murders of both Gloucester and Richard), and the comparisons in
the second half of the play between Richard and the crucified Christ.
Bolingbroke's proposed expiation for his Cain-like murder is a
pilgrimage to the Holy Land (V.vi.49–50); and there are other
references in the play to such pilgrimages and to Crusades, which
look forward to the *Henry IV* plays.

As we have already seen (Section 3.4 above), one recurrent theme
in the play is language and its relationship to reality. This is reflected
in the frequent references to language (breath, English, mouth, oath,
speech, tongue, word) and to lying and hypocrisy. There are also a
number of minor image-groups in the play: taste (sweet and sour,